Biography

PRODUCTOFMYENVIRONMENT
PART 2: THE JOURNEY TO ISLAM

Nicole Newman, President/CEO of Newman Networks is an inspiring motivational speaker, technology writer for the national on-line newspaper, The Examiner and exceptional business networker. She was born in Washington DC and grew up in the City of Brotherly Love, Philadelphia. She acquired a strong work ethic as a product of Julia R. Reynolds Masterman School and the George Washington Carver High School of Engineering and Science.

Nicole started her college career at the University of North Carolina at Greensboro. In her second year, she was involved in a car accident that left her with a broken femur bone and a sublegal hematoma to the brain. Although she was unable to complete school at the University of NC at Greensboro, 2 months later while on crutches she transferred to Temple University and graduated magna cum laude from the Fox School of Business with a Bachelors of Business Administration in Risk Management and Insurance, Management Information Systems and a minor in Human Resources. She went on to complete her MBA at the

1

prestigious Robert H. Smith School of Business at the University of Maryland majoring in Finance.

She started her professional Information Technology career at CIGNA where she found a niche in database design and reporting. She was fascinated by putting data in a sequence that built information. After a 15 year run, she ended her corporate career at the global consulting firm of Deloitte Touche Tomatsu. She learned intrapreneurship skills from the Chief Learning Officer, Nick Van Dam founder of the non-profit organization e-learningforkids.org. She used that knowledge to pursue her passion in entrepreneurism and bridging the digital divide. Nicole started Newman Networks, a Pennsylvania and Delaware certified M/WBE firm, in April of 2006 she owned diversephilly.com, a website for businesses to share the costs of advertising. In just the second year, the company quadrupled revenue. With 2000 Linkedin connections, 6000 Facebook friends and 80 testimonials, the company made a massive network in the local marketplace. This is just one of the testimonials – "Nicole Newman is an outstanding individual. She is an incredible connector and exemplifies in her daily life the proof that networking is the key to building a successful business. Nicole cares most about her clients, colleagues and friends; assisting them in building strong relationships that will lead to company growth and success. Anyone doing business in the Greater Philadelphia region should get to know Nicole immediately. She will absolutely take your business to the next level." from Kate Bay, former Regional Account Executive, Greater Philadelphia Chamber of Commerce.

Now you can find Nicole hosting monthly networking events in addition to her second passion of writing technology articles. Nicole is a former member of the Greater Philadelphia Chamber of Commerce and current member of The Power Lunch Project. She was recently honored by the NAACP for being one of 2012's Most Influential African American Women, The 2011 Madam CJ Walker Award presented by the National Coalition of 100 Black Women (Pennsylvania Chapter) and The Business Center's 2010 Awardee for Best Practices in Creative Marketing, in addition to The Philadelphia Tribune's 10 under 40 to watch of Influential African Americans and the Urban Momentum's 2009 Networker of the Year.

She is also a single mom of three children ages 12, 10 and 9 and resides in the West Philadelphia section of the city.

A Dedication to My M's

We all know that words can be used to hurt or used to heal. My religion teaches that most sins committed by people are sins of the tongue. I have witnessed words that forever scared a child all the way into adulthood or transformed thinking for an entire lifetime that affected multiple generations.

I recently read *"The word "no" is heard with great frequency in our everyday lives. As adults we find ourselves dealing with "no" on a regular basis. For example: "No, there are no tables without a reservation" or "No, you have to wait your turn" or even "No, we are out of that brand." There are signs all over our landscape with messages that read "no smoking," "no parking" or "no skateboards." The word "no" is just a fact of life for us all."*

But in my youth, I questioned everything. I was not raised to accept no. My follow-up question was "why not?" and my mother took the time to explain but sometimes the answer would be "life is not fair."

As you will read in this book, I was brought up in a very positive home environment with family speaking words of wisdom on a daily basis. Those positive words were extremely beneficial growing up in the semi-rough neighborhoods of Philadelphia. This book is dedicated to my mom and second mom, my mentor and the many mentors and writers who used the power of their words to allow me to dream bigger dreams that someday this little girl from West Philadelphia could make a mark on this world to change my mother's answer of "life is not fair," to an answer that means "life is fair" regardless of economic status, gender, race, creed, color or religion In sha Allah (God Willing)

(Source: http://voices.yahoo.com/best-parenting-advice-ever-saying-no-children-226255.html)

Why I Write?

Dear Daughter,

As you make the transition to womanhood, this can be a very confusing time. I have tried to shield you from television so you can stop witnessing women showing their bodies to get attention and African American boys disrespecting themselves by their treatment of young women. I know you can hear the cursing and swearing out here on the streets. I have attempted to show you different. Though we had a late start on the righteous path, it was a start none the less. To have something different, I must start and take the journey because I want different for you. The vicious cycle of single motherhood didn't start with me but I fight to make sure YOU have different choices. As I reflect upon my choices, I chose the path of least resistance. I chose the path of ease and I am paying the price for choosing to be a single mom. It is not the path to order and structure and the much needed foundation to raise children out the dunya (this world) to clearly see the beauty of the deen (the act of submission to God).

I am still struggling but I have learned a few things over the past few years. Your journey to find your help mate begins with someone who respects you for your good qualities and your not so good qualities. The help mate is looking to make you a better wife, a better mother AND a better person. He is your cover and you are his cover. So, whenever he is speaking badly about another person know he has the capacity to speak badly about you. They say "you attract what you are" so it is in your best interest in many ways to spend your time working to make you better. I have seen more than a few people get married for fear of a man being taken by someone else. I need you to understand and believe in the Qadr. If Allah willed it for you to have it then you would have it. If he went with someone else then it is his loss for he is not worthy of you.

One of your most valuable assets is your innocence and no man deserves it who is not willing to go through the marriage process to get it. Boys (not men) will try you hard to take away your assets but it is your job to trust the laws of our religion that govern our affairs and turn to your family for additional guidance. Have patience to perform your obligations and avoid the sins. You come from generations of strong, seemingly independent women and the vicious cycle stops with you and me In sha Allah.

Table of Quotes

Lessons Learned from Mom's

1. "It doesn't pay to get a C." – quoted by Ms. Cynthia Moultrie
2. You can kill more bees with honey than you can with a fly swatter." - quoted by My Mom
3. "You can be anything you want to be." - quoted by My Mom
4. "We are not poor, we are broke...know the difference." - quoted by My Mom
5. "The decision maker does not sit in the big chair, but the desk in front of the big chair." - quoted by My Mom
6. "Don't defecate where you eat." - quoted by author unknown, told by My Mom
7. "You must forgive yourself." - quoted by My Mom
8. "It is just easier to do the right thing." - quoted by My Mom
9. "If a person is not positioned to tell you YES, then they are also not positioned to tell you NO." - quoted by My Mom
10. "Dress for the job you want NOT the job you have." - quoted by My Mom
11. "Less Is More." - quoted by Nicole Newman, a lesson for her daughter
12. "The quicker you realize you can't do it all, the better.

Surpassing limits is growth." - quoted by Nicole Newman

13. "Who are you to judge?" - quoted by Nicole Newman as a lesson for her daughter

14. Learn to EARN not ask." - quoted by Nicole Newman, a lesson for her daughter

15. To effect CHANGE on the outside we must begin the process from WITHIN." - quoted by Nicole Newman, a lesson for her daughter

Lessons learned from Mentors

16. "Successful people realize that we become who we hang around.... and hang around who they want to become." - quoted by Donna Krech

17. "Marketing is belief in yourself transferred to someone else." - quoted by My mentor, Sulaiman Rahman

18. "Don't try to make people respect your reasoning, just give them no choice but to respect your results." - quoted by Sulaiman Rahman

19. "The only constant is change, and changes constantly." - quoted by Marcus Williams III.

20. "Everyone has a deadline, they just don't know what it is." - quoted by Tara Colquitt

21. "Success is belief in yourself, belief in your product and belief in the system." - quoted by My mentor, Mr.

Sulaiman Rahman

22. "It is not what you know (because that is why you went into business), it is what you don't know that makes it too much." - quoted by Tara Colquitt

23. "Gratitude is like a currency. Many debts have been satisfied by a sincere gesture of it" quoted by Sulaiman & Celia Rahman

24. "Labels are for products, not for people." - quoted by my highly respected friend, Camari Ellis

25. "When everything is going wrong, that's when you know you are on the right path. Good things come to those who wait." - quoted by my mentor, Sulaiman Rahman. I will add -- with good intentions.

26. "You are only a true entrepreneur if you only make money from your efforts." – quoted by Tara Colquitt

27. "Everything you want is on the other side of FEAR #getoverit." – quoted by My mentor, Sulaiman Rahman

Lessons learned from Mistakes

28. "Giving people self-confidence is by far the most important thing that I can do. Because then they will ACT." - quoted by Jack Welch.

29. "If you are your authentic self, you have no competition." - quoted by Author Unknown

30. "Children learn more from who you are than what you

teach." - quoted by W.E.B. Du Bois

31. "Success isn't measured by money or power or social rank. Success is measured by your discipline and inner peace." - quoted by football coach and legend, Mike Ditka

32. "How you do anything is how you do everything." - quoted by Author Unknown

33. "No one can make you feel inferior without your consent." - quoted by former First Lady, Eleanor Roosevelt

34. "Successful and unsuccessful people do not vary greatly in their abilities. They vary in their desires to reach their potential." - quoted by leadership author, John Maxwell

35. "All business is personal." - quoted by Barry Schwartz

36. "Time is Money." - quoted by Benjamin Franklin

37. "Some men can run the fastest, jump the highest, or lift the heaviest, but no man has the corner on ambition, desire, and hustle." - quoted by Author Unknown

38. "Plans are nothing; *planning is everything."* - quoted by Dwight D. Eisenhower

39. "Wealth is a state of mind." - quoted by Author Unknown

40. "Leadership is Influence. To influence you must learn the rules of two-way communication." - quoted by John

C. Maxwell

41. "Business is a Marathon, Not a Sprint." - quoted by Author Unknown

42. "I don't care how much power, brilliance or energy you have, if you don't harness it and focus it on a specific target, and hold it there you're never going to accomplish as much as your ability warrants." - quoted by Zig Ziglar

43. "Communication is Key." - quoted by Author Unknown

44. "Word is bond." - quoted by Author Unknown

45. "Though no one can go back and make a brand new start anyone can start from now and make a brand new ending." - quoted by Carl Bard.

46. "People quit their boss, not their job." - quoted by Author Unknown

47. "No man is an Island." - quoted by Michael Gerber, author of the e-Myth Revisited

48. "We are kept from our goal not by obstacles but by a clear path to a lesser goal." - quoted by Robert Brault

49. "You go, we go." - quoted by Kurt Russell in Backdraft

50. "Happiness is when what you think and what you do and what you say are congruent." - quoted by Mahamta Ghandi

51. "If you want to live a happy life tie it to a goal not to people or things." - quoted by Mahamta Ghandi

52. "Opportunity is missed by most people because it is

dressed in overalls and looks like work." - quoted by
Thomas Edison

53. "Many hands make light work." - quoted by John
Heywood

54. "When there is no enemy within, the enemies outside
cannot hurt you." - quoted by Author Unknown

55. "It's a lot about raising the bar, increasing your
expectations of yourself, to see yourself as a winner.
And part of that comes from earning the respect of
others through hard work." - quoted by Kris Thorson

Quote #1 "It does not pay to Get a C" - by Ms. Cynthia Moultrie, My second Mom

The scene starts sometime in March of the year 1990 in my final year of high school. Ms. Cynthia, my second mom, was driving me home from my BFF's house in southwest Philadelphia. I had just received my college acceptance letter from the University of North Carolina at Greensboro. I was super excited as my BFF, her daughter, was also going to school in North Carolina just up the road at North Carolina Central University. "You know" she said "it doesn't pay to get a C in college, YOU are paying for your grades." I just sat there, trying to comprehend what she was saying.

This was a shocking statement as I was already an economics major studying with my online teacher, Dr. Julianne Malvaeux at CNN University that aired on Sunday mornings. This was before online distance learning, actually this was before the mainstream internet phenomenon. What I heard is that I was losing money by obtaining a grade lower than a B. In other words, if I wanted a positive return on the dollars I was spending for college, my class grade had better be at least a B.

23 years later, I still remember what she said like it was yesterday. My commitment level to not only go to college as that was my mother's plan but now I wanted to excel in my

studies at college. I was going to school out of state, I did not formally have financial aid package until school had actually began. Luckily, I did not have the freshman selection of courses. Let's just say my favorite class was Mythology instead of English 101 like the rest of the freshman class. My first semester I came home with 2 C's, 2 B's and a A in my favorite class, Mythology. I was disappointed in myself. My GPA was a dismal 2.8, in other words, I lost money. I knew what it felt like to perform below expectations and I wanted to not have that feeling ever again. The mistake I see many parents make, including myself, is rewarding children for outcomes. What we should strive for is to reward children for effort. We need to connect the dots that effort helps determine outcome i.e. more effort for a better outcome.

The second semester I buckled down and focused on school work while training for the Resident Assistant Program. I finished the semester with 3 A's, 3 B's and a 3.5 grade point average and achieved the goal of becoming a Resident Assistant. After the dismal first semester and wonderful second semester, my grade point average improved to a 3.27. In other words, I was now making money on the $20,000 annual college investment!

What I learned years later in network marketing is that there are four types of motivating factors for people - financial, helpful, popular and self motivated. Every person has all of these factors but one usually dominates. At that time, I was motivated by financial goals. What my second mom did for me was spoke about grades in financial terms. No one had ever done that before. She connected the dots and spoke the language that motivated me to move into action.

Those are the powerful words that I used as motivation, along with a couple Facebook friends, to write this book. In this community, I see too many people who use the power of words to hurt one another through the various sins of the tongue called cursing, gossiping, back biting, etc. I am continuously learning to train my tongue to speak positively about myself and others with the hope that we, as a people, understand the power of words and use them to heal each other and move out of complacency into action. Words are powerful but the result of the words is action.

The difference I see in myself as I matured is that I am no longer motivated by financial goals. I had to learn that money cannot buy happiness. Happiness comes from living with integrity and learning how to be a better person along the righteous path. Bruce Lee said "The measure of the moral worth of a man is his happiness. The better the man, the more the happiness. Happiness is the synonym of well-being." I have changed from being motivated by financial goals to helping people. I am motivated to help people who want to be helped. This is such a blessing Alhamdulillah, which means all praise is due to Allah! We are seizing the opportunity to financially benefit the community by sharing the knowledge which is a form of helping people. Now, I try get every young person's ear to say the exact same words that my second mom said to me 23 years ago -- "it doesn't pay to get a C in college, YOU are paying for your grades."

Quote #2 "You can kill more bees with honey than you can with a fly swatter." – My Mom

This lesson I am still learning. My mother is the writer in the family. If you have good understanding of the English language then a person can resolve an issue with words. Anger is a product of not being able to express emotions through the use of words. They say "Kind words and good manners will open more doors than an angry attitude!" People use emotions because it is true, what they say "The loudest person gets the most attention"

I am usually the loudest person, which is why I am still trying to learn this lesson. I am looking for balance between getting the attention and resolving the issue with words. My attitude shows that I want attention NOW then I have to turn off the switch and use kind words and good manners to resolve the issue with words.

It pays to remember what they say, "ATTITUDE is EVERYTHING…"

Quote #3 "You can be anything you want to be."

.My mother said "you can be anything you want to be" in our non-Muslim home. Although she said it, I didn't really believe her until I was 15 and made a complete mess of my blessings. My mother said to me, you made this mess so YOU clean it up. At the time I had no money, no internet, no cell phone but Alhamdulillah the mess I made was cleared. Then I believed her. Now I tell my children that they can be what Allah has blessed them to be. Set goals and discipline yourselves to work the plan daily! Is it time for me to take my own advice.

Quote #4 "We are broke not POOR - there is a difference."

I grew up, like most Philadelphians, living in a one bedroom apartment but I saw my mother "move us on up" every couple of years. I have a picture of me and my mom unpacking groceries and in the picture is the white box with the blue label. It was the Money Saving Brand detergent. Even though we did not always have a lot of money she reminded me that "we were broke not POOR, there is a difference." Poverty is a mindset. Financial Social Work says "The Poverty Mindset is built upon a foundation of negativity." People with a poor mindset are always looking for ways not to spend money and "get over" on other people. This type of person cannot have an "attitude of gratitude." For example, because they do not have everything they think they need, they feel like they have nothing, or have lost it all. This of course is just a mindset, a mentality. Henry Ford said "Whether you think you can, or you think you can't – you're right." Negative thinking makes negative outcomes. If people think they can't have a better financial future, they are unlikely to try to learn how to or to even consider putting in the effort. Grace Under pressure Blog says "When you begin to work with the poor, you will find yourself frustrated at their lack of initiative, their giving up as soon as they hear any kind of negative answer. Their inertia. Part of that is that for most of the poor, life has been one long beat down. It is not like they up and decided at 21 to be poor and "losers," as we might be apt to call them. It started in childhood. It started in their parents' and grandparents' childhood. They learned early that things don't work out. That there is not much point in saving money because it will get soaked up by some "emergency" later on. You might as well spend it now because you need it now.

They learn very quickly that they are different. It is both enraging and heartbreaking to go with a poor family to any kind of social services or hospitals. Too often, they are treated rudely, treated as if they are stupid. After spending some time and building some trust with one family, both parents let out that they did not like going anywhere that might help them because they always come back feeling badly about themselves. It is deep."

Financial Social Work wrote[4], "Poverty is culturally endemic, systemic and inter-generational. It is the result of many complex factors, circumstances and issues with no single or simple solution. However, financial education and asset building have become a significant and accepted approach for lifting people above the poverty line. While financial knowledge is certainly an important component of financial literacy such an approach tends to ignore how a person's thinking impacts his/her ability to integrate and adapt new information into their life. In this case, it is the Poverty Mindset which determines that ability and influence the degree of success which can be achieved.

In other words, it is a person's thoughts, feelings and attitudes about money which is the foundation of how that person relates to money and is the heart of their relationship with money. It is an individual's relationship with money that drives their financial behavior – financial behavior (how a person earns, spends, saves and shares) ultimately determines their financial circumstances."

Dani Johnson writes[5] about how to break the mindset:

"1. Your Environment Is Everything

Sue grew up on welfare with parents who ran out of money continuously – then used what money they did have for drugs. There was abuse, no peace, and no security. Growing up in that environment absolutely shapes one's mind about money and life. There was no budgeting to help make their money last; they would blow it all on junk food, alcohol and drugs – then act like victims until the next check arrived. Change your environment – change your financial future.

2. Do not Speak The Language Of Poverty

How many hours do we spend in school learning financial wisdom? Zero! So, where do you learn your financial habits? From other adults, mainly your parents. If your parents spent foolishly, their actions taught you to spend foolishly. If your parents spent wisely, you would gravitate towards wisdom in finances. Sue grew up with the language of poverty that sounds like "we can not afford it," or "we do not have the money" or "that is for rich people, not us." All those statements are victimized, poverty statements. Change your language, and you change your financial future.

3. Eliminate Unhealthy Financial Traditions

Unhealthy traditions pass from one generation to the next. They say "repetition is the mother of learning." Through repetition you learned poor financial skills; through repetition you will learn great financial skills. Beware who you learn from. You should learn from someone who has a lot of money – not just someone who looks the part. Most people are far from reaching their goal of financial independence. Change your traditions, and you change your financial future.

A Poverty Mindset evolves over time – it is not something anyone is born with. It is something that is formatively learned and experienced." Which means today is as good a day as any to do something different, make the intentions, put the intention into action and repeat daily to get different results.

Quote #5 "The decision maker does not sit in the big chair, but the desk in front of the big chair."- by My Mom

What she meant is the secretaries, administrative assistants, the help, etc.. are the gatekeepers AND the decision makers. There are some people who believe titles mean power. I am not that type of person because of the wisdom my mother shared with me. What is valuable to me is the information people, not titles, hold. The person with the information might have the title or they might not.

The movies from back in the day (i.e. Gone With the Wind and other historical movies) showed butlers, maids and nannies being in the room but paid no mind. The people talking totally ignored these groups of people like a fly on the wall (with ears). The information was transmitted from these so called flies to people who wanted access to the information. This is still true today. They say "a test of a man's character is how he treats people that can do nothing for him." That means a man/woman has judged the people who can do nothing for him. That is exactly why I do not operate using that mindset. I say "everyone has value" so no one gets treated any better because they have a title and no one is treated with the "paid no mind" attitude because they don't have a title. Everyone has done something for someone else even if that something was just a smile.

I am a giver by nature but over time I learned how to become a calculated giver MashaAllah. Life has shown me that the person I give to will not be the person who I receive from. Since I don't know where my next blessing is coming from, I make it easy on myself and give to those who know how to show appreciation. People who don't show appreciation to others are takers so I don't have to waste time, energy and resources by giving to them. I can deal with them on a different level. I can usually write off takers with this quote "The only people worthy of your time are those willing to pay for it." Takers do not operate as givers so they tend to hoard their resources (money or time) so they get nothing in return.

In general, the administrative assistants, janitors, maintenance people, nannies, etc. are used to being overlooked so any act of kindness is taken seriously. It is in my best interest and my companies best interest to give generously to those groups of people because they have access to information (by being a fly in the room) that is valuable. You might wonder how is the administrative assistant the gatekeeper and the decision maker? Now, I share the lesson my mom shared with me. For the decision maker to make a decision, they must see the request. The request comes through the gatekeeper (administrative assistant) who makes a decision to pass or not pass the information along. So, the gatekeeper is making a decision on whether the request is even worthy of getting to the next step. In this example, let's say the request is passed along.

If the gatekeeper wants the request to get approved, they can put the request in front of the decision maker and simply say - sign here. If they want the request to be denied, they can also provide the request and the details with a couple of statements that include their opinion and usually the request is denied right there. That is why mom said "The decision maker does not sit in the big chair, but the desk in front of the big chair."

When we think about giving it does not have to be big. If a person can show appreciation they will return with a smile whether the gift is big or small. Random acts of kindness could simply be a smile, a hello, an acknowledgement or my favorite, a small token of appreciation. Over time, random acts of kindness are quite influential on how the requests are presented to the decision maker. As any marketer will tell you, "presentation is key."

Now that I have shared my mother's wisdom, you have been empowered. They say "knowledge is power" and with my job I am blessed to "EMPOWER YOU!" Now it is your turn "empower someone else" to pay it forward by giving back.

Quote #6 "Don't defecate where you eat." - by Author Unknown, told to me by My Mom

Don't defecate where you eat is the same version of the more friendly saying - "Don't dip your pen in the company ink." This means be careful when it comes to getting involved with people who you have to see on a continual basis what they call "workplace romances." Break ups are easier when the person is out of sight, out of mind. Psychology Today author Sean Horan defines[6] "workplace romances" as "A workplace romance is considered a relationship that occurs "between two members of an organization where sexual attraction is present, affection is communicated, and both members recognize the relationship to be something more than just professional and platonic. Workplace romances are commonplace. Statistics indicate that anywhere from 40-47% of employees surveyed had been involved in a workplace romance. Beyond the 47% involved, about 20% indicated they were receptive to an office romance." The author goes on to say "All romantic relationships are complicated, but office romances present unique challenges in that you spend more time with your co worker/romantic partner and need to, simultaneously, manage the perceptions of other co workers. Those who enter into workplace romances should be aware of the workplace implications and challenges that such relationships present."

I see all type of warning signs for women getting involved in these types of relationships and why my religion strictly forbids this. Most relationships have a power structure. If one decides to partake in such relationship, it is the woman who is usually judged by the co-workers as the weak person in the relationship. She is judged as "giving in" and the evidence is that she got involved in the first place. They say "she gave in to his demands." This is a big loss of credibility. Credibility, i.e. reputation, means a whole lot as the reputation precedes people especially in business relationships.

The second warning is that men are worse than women when it comes to the gossip. Gossip for very good reasons is also forbidden in Islam for those to speak gossip and for those to listen to it. Now, the whole relationship has become the topic of conversation at the water cooler. Whatever secrets held between the people involved have now spread through the building faster than wildfire.

The third warning is the inevitable breakup. My mom used to say "if it starts off wrong, it will end wrong." The workplace (not home) is where people spend most of their time. Most workplace romances happen because of a physical need with a person or persons that people spend most of their time with. In other words, there is no goal to maintain the relationship past physical companionship. So, once the physical need is fulfilled, the parties usually go their separate ways and I hear the phrase "I'm done with her" and that is why the break-up is inevitable. The goal of the whole occurrence was a result of "short-term thinking." Short term thinking is a result of a small goal. The smaller the goal, the smaller the commitment to obtaining the goal. Just like the bigger the goal, the bigger the commitment level to obtaining the goal.

This whole situation can be avoided by "keeping your eye on the prize." To "keep your eyes on the prize" with focus and clarity, there must be a mission to obtain a goal. Personally, I can not think of a bigger goal than paradise but I recognize that all people are different so the question remains what is your goal? What are the action steps necessary to achieve the goal and what sacrifices will be made? The goal has to be not only spoken but written down so the goal becomes real since goals in the head are just dreams. There should also be a plan of action that can easily turn into milestones to maintain the commitment level. One person cannot be all things to all people so some sacrifices must be made. I sacrificed marriage as a goal shortly after college as I saw it as an impediment in the lives of most women. I know quite a few women who got "off track" by getting caught up in someone else's vision, like their husband or significant other, that was not their own. Although I sacrificed marriage, I did not sacrifice motherhood. I now see the error in my ways. My children's happiness and support system should not have been affected by the sacrifices made to achieve the goal.

The "company ink" stands a good chance of harming a woman's reputation because the goal came with no commitment and break-up is inevitable, it is worth it? That is why my mother warned me by saying "Don't defecate where you eat."

Quote #7 "You must forgive yourself." - by My Mom

The act of repentance is a beautiful blessing by the Creator. Before I embraced Islam, my mom used to tell me that I had to learn to forgive myself for all my mistakes. Some people walk around ashamed of what they have done but I have learned. I see mistakes as lessons and because I am human, I expect that I will make them and accept mistakes as lessons learned on the path to paradise. Being able to see the "silver lining" (lesson learned) in the rain cloud (mistakes) makes it easy to forgive myself. Since I am so transparent with the mistake, it becomes easy for me to share the lessons learned because I want my children and those I influence around me NOT to make the same mistake.

My mother also said "Being grateful for what you have and what you don't have opens the doorway to forgiveness." When you are internally happy (i.e. grateful) there is no need to hold others in contempt or seek vengeance to others. Positive Psychology News says[11], "Gratitude is complex. It is a positive emotion that can be cultivated with intentional activity. It is a character strength measured by the VIA Signature Strengths assessment. It is the foundation of a number of positive interventions that have been found to enhance happiness. Gratitude involves both acknowledging good things that happen – being mindful of present benefits – and recognizing that the sources of goodness are outside us.

Forgiveness is the flip side of gratitude. It involves responding positively to transgressions by offering mercy instead of vengeance. Like gratitude, it is outward directed and intentional and recognized as a VIA character strength." That is why people who are happy use forgiveness instead of vengeance as reactions to other people communication strategies. Sal Rachele says in the article Forgiveness and Gratitude[12], "If you are NOT experiencing a joyful, exciting, prosperous, loving life and meeting life's challenges with enthusiasm, then may I suggest that there is a deficiency in one of these areas. Either you have not forgiven yourself and others completely, or there is a lack of gratitude for all of life's lessons and experiences."

While it is important to forgive how does one do it? Step one, learn to forgive yourself. When one has learned to forgive themselves, in my religion it is done through the act of repentance, it is much easier to forgive others for their mistakes. Allah t'ala (Glorified and Exalted is He) is merciful. Here is the lesson learned from a Facebook friend – "An apology means nothing when you keep doing what you apologized for." Words without action mean nothing. The action requires change in behavior so that it does not happen again. Behavior only changes when people realize why they react to situations with certain behaviors. For example, Live Science wrote in their article[13], "Nobody knows for sure why humans lie so much, but studies find that it is common and that it is often tied to deep psychological factors."

"It is tied in with self-esteem," says University of Massachusetts Psychologist Robert Feldman. "We find that as soon as people feel that their self-esteem is threatened, they immediately begin to lie at higher levels." Unless the self-esteem problem is addressed, the behavior remains. Here is another one: "obesity" is tied to self-esteem. People who look at the issue as a health issue won't achieve results until the psychological not health problem is addressed.

Wikihow.com give steps on how to forgive. Step 1 (which is really Step 2) is "**Realize that the hate you feel toward your adversary does not harm him or her.** Resentment is like drinking poison and waiting for it to kill your enemy."

Step 2 (which is really Step 3) is **"Understand that the best revenge against your enemies is to live a successful and happy life.** Want to get even with someone who tried to destroy you? Show them and show yourself (and the world) that the obstacles they tried to build were not significant enough to disable you and/or destroy you."

Step 3 (which is really Step 4) and the one I use most often - **"Realize that the second best revenge is to turn the bad experience into something good, to find the proverbial silver lining in the dark cloud.** Think of your enemy as someone who has helped you to grow. Even though unfortunate things happen to us, the best thing we can do is take those opportunities as tests that will either destroy or strengthen us. If you've been *through* something, it didn't destroy you - take what you learned and become a better person because of it."

Then I skip a few steps to get to step 7 "**Learn that the Aramaic word for "forgive" means literally to "untie."** The fastest way to free yourself from an enemy and all associated negativity is to forgive. Untie the bindings and loosen yourself from that person's ugliness. Your hatred has tied you to the person responsible for your pain. Your forgiveness enables you to start walking away from him or her and the pain. Forgiveness is for you and not the other party. Freeing yourself through forgiveness is like freeing yourself from chains of bondage or from prison."

That is why forgiveness is along the same line as gratitude. Being unforgiving is being ungrateful and being forgiving is being grateful. We are blessed with another moment to live in the test we call life, we should all use it to forgive our fellow man and move along the journey free of the pain of an unforgiving heart.

At the Urban League Small Business Matters event, Ed Gordon said, "Business is not a question of will I fail but WHEN will I fail. What happens next is your choice." Businesses like everything else must adapt to change. Barry Ritzhold, a Capital Analyst on the Ritzhold Blog[14], noted that "the success rate of small business in year one is just 15%, the success rate in year 2 doubles to 30%, the success rate in year 3 jumps to 38% and the success rate steadily climbs as the business matures. Businesses that make it through the first few years have a much greater chance of success. Lack of experience is the most important cause of failure and is often the cause of failure reasons 2 through 10." If a business owner has never managed anything before it is going to be very hard to manage a business. If a business owner is not process driven, it will be very difficult to put processes in place. If a business owner is afraid of commitment then the owner most likely will not use their resources to hire staff and take the risks to grow the business.

Hiro Boga, a noted business coach says[15], "To grow your business, you must grow yourself. Business growth is anchored in personal growth the way a tree's roots are anchored to the ground that nourishes it." Business expansion brings increased risk and complexity as well as the potential for outstanding rewards – and it requires an expanded version of you to shape and hold it. The most successful of my clients are those who understand this. They willingly cultivate a loving relationship with their soul and with the essence of their business. Their business flourishes, serving them, the people and causes they love, while shaping a world that works for everyone. Much of the work my clients and I do together is about building capacity – the capacity to handle risk; to ride the waves of uncertainty without losing focus and commitment to their deepest desires. The capacity to reshape identities, transform beliefs, and evolve into the inner pattern of their being. The capacity to partner effectively with the soul of their business and to manage increasing complexity in their business relationships." In other words, those business owners who fail to change limit their personal growth which limits their vision and most likely leads to failure in their business. A business owner cannot and should not stay the same in the quickly changing business environment.

There are many technical aspects to a business like doing great market research, developing a product, understanding technology, doing competitive analysis, product positioning, pricing strategy, finance, and on and on. These "technical" business skills are critically important, and we all need to continuously learn them. But when it comes down to being successful, you'll find that people skills are really the most important of all. Every decision, project, program, negotiation, or sale comes down to people interacting with each other. And as most executives understand, every single decision we make has uncertainty and a "gut feel" associated with it (even those which are informed by lots and lots of data). Business is about interacting with people. Like Bob Burg famously said in his bestselling book, Endless Referrals, "All things being equal, people do business with people they know, like and trust." This is true for big business which is why McDonalds, Target and other brands train their staff and it is especially true in small business.

We know that most businesses fail. The question is what

happens next? Change is a must and businesses have to reinvent themselves. My business started in the biggest recession the United States had seen in over 50 years. When the economy slows down, businesses for some very strange reason stop marketing in a desperate attempt to cut down on expenses. The number of clients who could afford my services quickly dried up. Since I was new and "wet behind the ears," I pressed on. That persistence and the blessings of Allah t'ala sent MULTIPLE opportunities my way. My company secured our first contract with the Hospital of the University of Pennsylvania and I got involved in network marketing. One can not grow their self by their self. My mentor took me and hundreds of other folks under his wing so we could go through the personal growth system. For me, network marketing was a personal development plan with a compensation model attached. I knew internally that I did not have the people skills (Bob Burg's book helped me) to be successful in business. I refused to pay for more education so network marketing offered me an opportunity that I did not want to miss! My confidence grew during that time as I found customers willing to pay for services and completed my second 26.2 mile marathon. I changed myself and my business grew. Now the answer to the question, what happens next becomes simple. How bad do you want to grow or stay in business? Are you willing to change? #thechoiceisyours

Quote #8 "It is just easier to do the right thing" - by My Mom, a lesson for her daughter

Doing the right thing involves making a choice. You have two choices, one will be the right thing to do according to either your moral compass or your religious beliefs. The other choice is to do what you want to do regardless of who it hurts or what you know is right.

Peter F. Drucker said "Management is doing things right; leadership is doing the right things." What I have found is that the "right" thing is subjective. One person thinks doing XXX is right and another person thinks doing YYY is right. Since we have been brought up by a different sets of rules and guides, this is bound to happen. Danwald Schmidt wrote[24], "It is important to remember how important making the right decision really is. The truth is that what your life becomes is a direct result of all the stressed-out, painful short-term decisions you make each and every day. Each decision contributes to the results that you will realize one day.

If you make the wrong decisions consistently — even small ones — you will end up with results that are embarrassing and expose you to be the fraud that you really were all along. If you consistently take the "easy way" and pursue shortcuts in the hope of "getting rich quick," then you'll find yourself in a future where you continue to be poor — mentally and financially. If you blame others for your mistakes and refuse to make corrections or learn from bad decisions that you have made in the past, then the results of your life will only be misery and arrogance."

You will become the person you decide to be. Which is why doing the right thing is always the right thing to do. Because doing the wrong thing molds you into the type of person that you don't want to be.

Herek Edberg of the Positivity Blog wrote[25], "Why should you do the right thing? Here are three excellent reasons:

1. You tend to get what you give.

By doing the right thing you tend to get the same things back. Give value to people, help them and they will often want to help you and give you value in some form. Do the right thing, put in the extra effort and you tend to get good stuff back. Don't do it and you tend to get less good stuff back from the world.

2. To raise your self-esteem.

When you don't do the right thing you are not only sending out signals out into your world. You are also sending signals to yourself. When you don't do the right thing you don't feel good about yourself. It is like you are letting yourself down. You are telling yourself that you can't handle doing the right thing.

3. To avoid self-sabotage.

A powerful side effect of not doing the right thing is that you give yourself a lack of deservedness. This can really screw up you and your success. So you start to self-sabotage, perhaps deliberately or through unconscious thoughts."

In the Islamic marriage, religion is used as the guide to what is "right" with the husband making the final decision that is aligned to the religious rules. This helps everyone "get on the same page" as to what is right. Maybe there is hope that I can finally do the right thing and get married In sha Allah. My children will learn more from what I show them than what I teach.

Quote #9 "If a person is not positioned to tell you YES, then they are also not positioned to tell you NO." - by My Mom

The article, Best Parenting Advice Ever Said to Children says[20], "The word "no" is heard with great frequency in our everyday lives. As adults we find ourselves dealing with "no" on a regular basis. For example: "No, there are no tables without a reservation" or "No, you have to wait your turn" or even "No, we are out of that brand." There are signs all over our landscape with messages that read "no smoking", "no parking" or "no skateboards." The word "no" is just a fact of life for us all." But in my youth, I questioned everything. I was not raised to accept no.

My job as a business owner is to close sales and let my contractors do the work. To close sales, I have to know my ratio - for every 1 yes, we average 4 no's and no means "Not Now." I am sharing what my mother told me that made working with other people much easier - "If a person is not positioned to tell you YES, then they are also not positioned to tell you NO." Titles mean NOTHING. The person that controls the money IS the decision maker. She also told me the gatekeepers (administrative assistants, cooks, janitors, etc.) have power. They get the information first and can either choose or choose not to share it. To avoid the middlemen, first recognize who is the decision maker by honoring the relationships with the people with power (administrative assistants, cooks, janitors, etc.). For example, when I started my business I was marketing with cold calling. One the first call, I was not trying to make a sale. My objective was to get to the decision maker. One easy technique is to utilize linkedin.com to find the right person (i.e. the decision maker) at the company. Once that person is identified, use cold calling and ask for the person's e-mail address from the gatekeeper. This keeps it simple for the gatekeeper by giving them one less person to worry about and helped me get to my objective - an audience with the decision maker that avoids the middle men.

In his article "No really means not now" Jerry Kennedy said that[21], "First and most important, you must master the proper mindset. Why? Developing the right mindset helps you handle the inevitable rejection involved in selling for a living (and business owners sell to generate revenue for their business). It is because they know this little secret: No does not really mean no—it just means not now."

If you're talking to a prospective customer (and if he's not a prospect, why are you talking to him in the first place?), the fact that he tells you no does not suddenly turn him into a non-prospect, does it? Of course not. It just means you were not able to either uncover his triggers and present the right solution or connect with him on some level. When the people with power lead me to the decision maker, they make it easy and position the opportunity as a win win scenario with a choice. The decisions can only be Yes, the prospect is in or

No, the prospect is not. Whether the answer is Yes or No, your company has gained a client, knowledge, or their time win. Your company has won because they have either secured a new partner or found out new information for the relationship or they are not interested in your company's services saving you valuable time. Even if you hear NO, understand "No" just means "Not Now."

Jerry Kennedy also said "In the meantime, move on. This is not the end of the world. Put this prospect back in the queue and check in with him periodically to see if circumstances have changed." From a marketing perspective, when the systems are in place for follow up and the triggers are hit, the prospect will come back to your business because they are now aware of the services offered by your company. Now your company is in a Yes or No position with the prospect and that is the objective.

Quote #10 "Dress for the job you want NOT the job you have"
- by My Mom

My mom always said dress for the job you want NOT the job you have because "A leader leads by example, whether he intends to or not." Define yourself by the blessings and use those talents to serve.

"Regardless of how you feel inside, always try to look like a winner. Even if you are behind, a sustained look of control and confidence can give you a mental edge that results in victory." - by former Wimbledon winner, Arthur Ashe

Kelly Azevedo wrote in theglobeandmail.com that[22], "For women leaders, business can be a minefield of personal image challenges. Experts estimate that up to 95 percent of our communication is nonverbal, so even as women achieve more prominent platforms, the majority of what we communicate is still through external visual clues. This builds the very real challenge of authentically aligning the messages we speak to our outer appearance. The appearance of a job or political candidate, business partner or clients impacts our opinions, whether we acknowledge it or not. While we still have strides to make in gender equality, many women are discovering that their outward appearance may have unintended consequences.

In an ideal world, all leaders would be evaluated by their effectiveness and character. However, seemingly innocent choices impact the influence of powerful women leaders across many fields. For the female executive, it is an added layer to be considered in developing an authentic leadership style — the fact is, as a professional woman, wearing inappropriate attire can undermine your authority.

Just look at the political field, where the power and perception of women is still heavily influenced by their outward appearance. Margaret Stuntz-Tresky's thesis "Clothing Makes the Candidate?" posts that "media coverage that underscores traditional sex roles or highlights women's gender or appearance may well contribute to and exacerbate these inherent hurdles to power."

Stuntz-Tresky compiled decades of research to exhibit that "studies in a variety of fields and settings have demonstrated that clothing has a significant influence on perceptions of trustworthiness, expertise, knowledge, intelligence, success and more — all the makings of source credibility."

The way we dress goes beyond fashion to what The Style Concierge Sybil Henry calls "personal style" — i.e., the way we dress to represent our authentic selves, so we can attract those who appreciate who we are internally. The challenge is to be taken seriously so that your message is heard and you don't lose that sense of personal authenticity.

As Henry notes, "when you work with a business, you sign on the dotted line to represent their brand and need to find a way to be authentic within those constraints. Choosing a company is no different than choosing a mate — you have to find a match in values and culture so you can authentically align yourself with the company values." When working with women executive or entrepreneurs, Henry helps identify her client's authentic self — and find a credible way to express that, comfortably and confidently. Corporate Image Coach Sarah Hathorn advises women "to allow their professional images to speak on their behalf — and beware of wardrobe choices that undermine her brand. Embodying your authentic brand is a process, but it sends a powerful statement and commands respect. In the end, it is not about conformity or mimicry, but identifying your authentic self and wearing it, inside and out, with confidence."

They say "Confidence is beautiful. No matter what your size, no matter what your weight, be confident in who you are and you will be beautiful." My mother always dressed to the 9's in her professional job. I remember three inch heels, silky legs and lots of curves. What she added when she became a business owner was braces in her thirties to enhance a million dollar smile. The first time I tried to embrace Islam I was wrongly turned away. The Muslim I asked to say my Shahadah (Islamic profession of faith) which means to embrace Islam through words told me that I need to cover my hair and wear shirts that covered my whole arm. I was not ready at that moment to make that seemingly drastic change in my lifestyle. I later learned that it was better to be embrace Islam and become Muslim (albeit a sinful Muslim) than live another day as a non-Muslim. A few months later I met another Muslim and I told him the story about wanting to be a Muslim. He called me the next day with this message "Go down on 60th street, get yourself a khimar, you are taking your shahadah." I said ok and was happy to finally be at peace with the alignment of my external appearance and my internal soul. In the beginning since I had so very little knowledge of Islam, I thought covering my hair was the only requirement. That is not the ^awrah (the body parts which must be covered from others) at all. Muslimahs need to be covered from head to toe with only the face (which does not include right under my chin or neck) and hands exposed. As I made the choice to submit to the will of Allah, I grew in confidence. Now my personal style benefits not only me but my business. That is the signature brand that identifies our distinct personality as I am usually the only Muslimah in the room. Alhamdulillah because that is beautiful.

Quote #11 "Less is More." - by Nicole Newman, a lesson for her daughter

I must say Darryl James put it so nicely in his post, "Overindulgence: The American Way[23]" that, "America's economy was stabilized after the Great Depression, with its citizens and leaders vowing never to go through such a horrible period of poverty again. Not only did the event demoralize Americans, it had destabilized the nation's economy, which meant that economic growth was hard to come by for America. But after WWII, America figured some things out. By assisting Europe in rebuilding itself through the Marshall Plan, it also made a number of foreign markets that were able (and felt obligated) to buy from America.

In the decades that followed, America began to experience wild economic growth. The benefits of that growth were passed on to youth, who, indulged in ways unlike their parents, began to view the world differently. By the Sixties, youth who had been indulged with things—televisions, cars, etc.—wanted something different. They chose to pursue a divergent lifestyle, which included drugs, wild music, and oh yes--sex, sex, sex. You see, they had been given all of the things that people previously had to work for and they did nothing to earn them. They were being taught that delaying gratification was unnecessary. We now see the results of decades of overindulgence, which includes a quickly descending value system and the never-ending pursuit of immediate gratification. We see this when kids won't wait until marriage for the wildest of sexual activities, or when young adults won't wait until achieving financial stability before purchasing expensive cars or taking lavish vacations.

In prior generations, every individual was necessary in order for the family to make it--even the children had to carry some of the weight. But when you enter into an era where there is excess and the children are not burdened with anything yet are indulged with everything, the result is an expectation of more of the same throughout life. The expectation of being overindulged is why relationships fail so often. One or both persons in the relationship expect to be overindulged, without a sense of having to do anything in return—not even to carry one's own weight. American women, who previously would have been preparing to cook, clean, mind the kids and do the sewing, still expect to be wined and dined, so that a man can demonstrate that he can provide for her. Most women aren't looking to be anything close to domesticated, but still expect the same privileges of financial demonstration. American men, who previously would have carried the sole financial burden for the family, still expect women to cook and to clean the house, demonstrating that the home would be tended to if the woman was provided for. Most men either aren't prepared to carry the burden single-handily, or simply have no clue as to what it truly means to be the standard bearer for a household, yet still expect the same privileges of domestic demonstration.

And, because Americans have become so lazy and selfish, even sitting down to have open and honest discussion about what is expected from the other is too much work. Americans who have been overindulged believe they deserve things, even though they have no idea what they should do to actually earn them. They look to others to fulfill their desires, because they have been brought up by parents and propaganda to believe that they are deserving of things simply because they exist in the world."

This post tells me what I am up against trying to raise a daughter to value herself, respect herself, show her that showing less skin is more beautiful, having less material possessions gives room for more gratitude, having less television i.e. someone else's vision gives her more vision. I am a product of the American environment though my mind has to see and want something else for both me and her.

Quote #39 "The quicker you realize you can't do it all, the better. Surpassing limits is growth." - by Nicole Newman

I like this quote even after I read and agreed with this quote from Bruce Lee, "If you always put limits on everything you do, physical or anything else, it will spread into your work and your life. There are no limits, there are only plateaus, and you must not stay there, you must go beyond them." It is important to note that most people are classified as to who they can be, what they can become and even their potential as children. I really think this thinking is not conscious. It is subconscious thoughts provided and passed down through the generations.

My mother was put ahead of her class at an early age by her teachers. When I was young, she told me that her music teacher was the one and only Roberta Flack. She graduated high school in 1971 at the end of the Civil Rights Movement when all types of opportunities were provided to African-Americans for the first time. As a result of the diversity initiative, my mother was accepted to the prestigious Bryn Mawr College on a full scholarship which included tuition, books, food, room and board. She was not limited in her opportunities and as a result, she instilled in me that I was not limited in mine.

Although sometimes I did not have belief in me, I knew without a shadow of a doubt that my mom had my back. The first team most of us are born into is our families. I say most of us because there are some families do not operate as a team.

They unconsciously (or consciously) put limits on themselves and their children.

From the time I became a woman until the age of 27, I was overweight. The doctors would try to explain to that I was obese but no one in my family would listen because everyone was overweight. They would say, she is just big boned like everyone else in the family. It was totally accepted that we can live with the health problem associated with obesity. Accepting the status quo is a huge LIMIT to change. Nobody made me feel inferior for being overweight and no one said it was a problem (like what we are saying unconsciously about premarital sex).

The first time I lost 40 lbs in college I actually did it by accident. We were living at 21st and Corinthian streets (near Girard College) while I was going to school at Temple University. It did not make a good financial sense to take SEPTA to Temple University which was only 1 subway stop away. So I walked to school every day. Over my senior year, I lost 40 lbs by accident. I knew walking was beneficial but I had no idea how beneficial it was.

I thought I was done because I had accomplished the goal. I lost the weight, graduated from college, and started working at CIGNA. What actually happened was that I gained it all back plus 10 lbs more! When I realized that my lifestyle changed, which helped me gain the weight back, I started walking again. This time it took me a few years of steady exercise and changing my lifestyle to attend graduate school at the University of Maryland at College Park where my first class did not begin until 9:30 a.m. The gym opened at 7am and I was there faithfully Monday, Wednesday and Friday. I know this is going to sound like a broken record but after I graduated from a different college (University of Maryland at College Park), I gained the weight back again this time it was a result of going through 4 pregnancies in a row.

My religion teaches knowledge before action. This time I accidentally sought knowledge from a knowledgeable teacher before engaging in action. Melanie Marchand owned a gym called SIS (Sisters In Shape) Fitness which offered a new beginners' class called the fitness challenge. This was an actual class with 2 midterms and a final. I failed the first midterm and did not win any awards in the contest. What I gained was knowledge needed to keep the weight off for 6 plus years and counting!

I thought I was limited to losing 40 lbs but I ended up losing 70 lbs by listening to my own quote "Know your limits... and SURPASS them." The morale of this story is that I was limited by my own knowledge which is why we need each other to teach and learn from. That is why I say "The quicker you realize you can't do it all, the better. Surpassing limits is growth."

Quote #13 "Who are you to judge?" - by Nicole Newman for her daughter

That quote meant I am not fit to judge.. I had a challenge with a young lady. I said to my daughter "I don't know what I'm going to do with her." She said, "You will do nothing. You will leave it up to Allah." The crabs in the barrel mentality try their best to take. That intention receives NO reward. I just looked at her and smiled. At 11 years old, she knows there is only one judge who gives the reward and delivers the punishment.

Quote #14 "Learn to EARN not ask." - by Nicole Newman a lesson for her daughter

When a woman asks and gets what she wants, she has won the battle but lost the war. Asking put her in a position of weakness (losing respect). If a woman chooses to earn (which is more difficult), she can get what she wants and earn respect. Earning requires knowledge, knowledge brings money, money brings power and power EARNS respect In sha Allah. That is why my mother taught me to earn NOT to ask. I have too much pride to ask Ma sha Allah

My world before Islam consisted of women who were driven to do something with their lives and all of the women I knew had skills. As I have learned, you attract what you are. My mom was successful in placing me in "an environment of success" at home and at school. Most of my friends were also children born to single working mothers with the exception of my Muslimah BFF and her sisters. Most of my friends went to college, like me and even the ones that did not go worked in a professional capacity. I was taught like my friends were taught to Earn NOT to ask. I did not even know that some women with a poor mindset expected men to provide for them until I embraced Islam. Today, I still find it incredibly difficult to ask or accept anything from a man. Some men have shown themselves to have ulterior motives other than correcting their intentions to give for the sake of Allah.

Men understand the power game very well while I am still

playing catch up. Unfortunately, some women choose not to rise above the game and partake in it. The game is summed up quite nicely in "Money. Power. Respect." People (and REAL MEN know this) first get the money, because money is the power and then you get the respect (from chicks and I say that because those are not REAL women). This crazy game only works on women who don't value what they have. Although in Philadelphia there are more women for eligible Muslim men by a way off margin, WOMEN ARE STILL THE PRIZE not the other way around. Eligible men are males who can afford to take on the responsibilities and the obligations a wife. When a woman goes into a marriage with the intention that she will be provided for, then she has fell for the game hook line and sinker. The woman has just sold herself to the highest bidder and men know this and use this information to their advantage. In other words, the woman has no money therefore she has no power and gets no respect. My mother and other mother's could not share that information with me because they also learned to EARN not to ask. Real women taught us to get the money first, with the money comes the power and therefore the respect. The drawback to knowing this information is that I cannot compete with women who don't value what they have.

Dedan Tolbert put it so eloquently on Facebook "Women have to make better decisions about who they sleep with." All religions say no sex before marriage and that is for the protection of the woman and the family. Women who give it up before marriage have lost their value!!! "Holding out on the goodies" holds men accountable to wanting to have a goal to get work to earn money and be eligible to afford a wife. That is why a virgin woman is much more valuable in a man's eye than a woman who is not a virgin. Women, including myself, have to place a higher value on ourselves by abstaining from sex until a worthy man is placed in our paths. That is the moral value the last two generations have not shared with our daughters. I used to think it that men were the cause of our self-destruction. Now, I place the blame squarely on myself for partaking in action without first acquiring knowledge. The benefit of knowing my mistake makes this a great lesson for my daughter.

Now, I can package both of these lessons to help my daughter and other daughters. Just like men who are working to afford a wife, women have to work to afford a husband. Women should be using their blessings to get the money AND hold onto their virginity. Then she is valuable both ways but still can't compete with women who don't value themselves which is a great thing Alhamdulillah!! Coco Chanel put it quite nicely in this quote - "In order to be irreplaceable, one must always be different." May Allah guide my daughter to be different and rise above the games Ameen.

Quote #15 "To effect CHANGE on the outside we must begin the process from WITHIN." – by Nicole Newman

They say "People are creatures of habit." They stay in a bad relationship because it is comfortable, they stay in the same job because it is comfortable, they live in the same neighborhoods because it is comfortable, they shop in the same stores because they are comfortable. Marketers, like me, use this knowledge to influence buying decisions. That is why the most sought after economic market are teenagers (ages 13-17). The proven theory goes that if you can hook them to a brand when they are a teenager, they stay with that brand for a lifetime.

I am living proof of that concept. When I moved back to Philadelphia from DC, I specifically moved to the neighborhood I grew up in and shop at the remaining neighborhood stores because we hold on to the memories of my youth. The owners might have changed but the familiarity usually brings back fond memories.

They say "The only way CHANGE happens is by people dissatisfied with the status quo" and my personal quote, "to effect CHANGE on the outside we must begin the process from WITHIN." A lot of people who are unhappy with the current situation look for change on the outside. It could be a temporary change like buying new possessions (clothes, shoes, cars) or a more permanent change like buying a house, moving to a different location but that is not really change.

That is a change of environment. If we really are unhappy with the situation, the mindset has to change in order to achieve different results. The say discipline is doing what you don't want to do when you don't want to do it" Humans do what they like to do and avoid doing what they don't like to do. The result of this behavior is the current condtions of a person's life. This means if they want to change the current conditions of a persons life they have to discipline themselves to do different behavior. That is why CHANGE is a function of discipline. The more we want to change, the more we want discipline.

Quote #16 "Successful people realize that we become who we hang around.... and hang around who they want to become like." - by Donna Krech

Donna Krech posted on Facebook "My son said "I've figured something out about myself Mom. I tend to become like who I spend the most time with. If they lay around, I lay around. If they eat junk, I eat junk. If they aren't goal oriented, I tend to not work on my goals."

Me-- "This is true for everybody Bud. As a man thinks, so is he. And we all tend to begin to think like those we hang around. Then our actions do the same thing. But most people go through their entire life and never come to this realization. This gives you the power to go do ANYTHING you want it life." (Yes... my kid is smart. It is Think for Success Thursday. Successful people realize that we become who we hang around.... and hang around who they want to become like."

My mentor would say "your income is the average of your five closest friends." Which implies, if you want to raise your income then get some new friends. The journey of my life was greatly influenced by my BFF's sister. At the impressionable age of 13, she went off to college. Although my mom had told me at a very young age that I was going to college, now I had a "frame of reference" to a beautiful young lady inside and out who actually went to college. Her sister and her other sister had become business owners in their own right with the support of their husbands. That set my expectation of how a

Muslim man is supposed to treat his wife. What I saw out of this "frame of reference" were men who did not just financially support their wives on a day to day basis but laid the foundation of business ownership for long-term success. This was almost twenty years ago and it is sad that these stories are few and far between but that is what I expect from my husband if I am blessed to have one and I will accept nothing less.

When I started the journey of business ownership in 2006 along with my five friends, two of them already had businesses and I was number three. In 2013, five of my friends have businesses and we are all waiting for number six to complete the circle. We were looking to change our income but we are not willing to give up our friendship. That's what happens when you have been friends almost as long as an entire life. In our teenage years, my friends and I would sit around and hold what we called "truth tables." We held rules that at the table we had to be completely honest about all our crazy adventures and how we felt about each other. In between talking about our adventures, we also talked about what goals we wanted to accomplish and what we were going to do as adults. In essence, we were setting goals for ourselves and planting seeds for future success but at the time we thought we were just having fun.

As we went through the transition to adulthood, just like I looked at my BFF's sister for inspiration, my friends and I looked at each other. I was blessed to become a homeowner right after I graduated college at the age of 22. They say "the younger you are to buy a house, the more financially wealthy you will be." Not long after that all my friends were buying houses and now all 6 of us are homeowners.

As I had the pleasure of working with my mentor, I took my BFF along for the ride and now she has her own business as a realtor 4 years later. They say "you are the average of your five closest friends" and "watch the company you keep." Why would I not want to be friends with women who inspire, support and love each other to reach our full potential for the sake of Allah?

Quote #17 "Marketing is belief in yourself transferred to someone else." – By My mentor and inspiration, Mr. Sulaiman Rahman

Forbes writer, Michael Brennan said in an article[3], **"The aim of marketing is to know and understand the customer so well the product or service fits him and sells itself." Quoted by Peter F. Drucker**

Marketing is not about who can talk faster or close better. It is about deep psychological understanding of customer needs. Steve Jobs had this gift better than almost any example. Henry Ford. Thomas Edison. Every innovation in the history of the world combined an uncanny understanding of human needs and the innovative vision to deliver it.

"Marketing is too important to be left to the marketing department." ~ Quoted David Packard

If business is composed of marketing and innovation, and marketing is about deep customer insights, then marketing is the job of every employee.

"Social Media" has only made this point painfully clear: every employee is an extension of the brand. The brand serves to meet the needs of the customer and the business serves to innovate.

Wir Sitzen Alle Im Marketing!

I'm not sure Google translator gave me the right translation but whether you are in finance, sales, marketing or the owner of a small business, *we are all in marketing*."

Exactly! Every facet of human interaction is a marketing activity to transfer belief in yourself to someone else. Someone else includes children, bosses, co-workers, family, husband, stores that are patronized, transportation, you name it. We market to get approval from our parents. We market to get into college. We market to find a mate. We market to get a job. We market to buy a car. We market to buy or sell a house. And we also market to find a customer for our business. If you ever had to talk to another person, you were marketing. Marketing is social interaction, social interaction is communication so instead of helping business owners market which they mistakenly think is selling, now I understand that I run a communications company with a goal of helping the business community (the target market) step out of their businesses to find strategic relationships (networking) in which to leverage assets (marketing) for win-win situations. In other words, the business community networks to cross market their products to consumers. The selfish, only child runs a communication company Alhamdulillah! amazing. Wow. This is where it gets very interesting. It is time for me to eat my own medicine. I am very blessed because I have been served enough humble pie in my life to enjoy the taste. Every time I take a bite, with the correct intention that it is good for me, I have gotten better and more focused on the goal. I have seen the lesson to make amends in many cases with a sincere apology or a sincere thank you and worked to make the relationship better. So, if I want to be a better person for the sake of Allah, I must eat more humble pie. As my teacher would say "it is good for you."

Over 80% of communication is non-verbal and the high usage of electronic mail and text messaging has made communication in many ways harder. E-mail is all verbal communication which means the non verbal communication gestures can not be used. The non verbal smiles and nods of the head for acknowledgement have to be translated to verbal form. This is where most people especially business owners fail. One time, I asked for feedback in an e-mail newsletter and a good friend responded with a long e-mail that I read but I did not acknowledge that I read or received it. The customer then stopped doing business with my firm because I did not acknowledge the communication. That is why they say "fortune is in the follow-up." It would have taken 2 minutes to respond with – we have received your communication and are addressing your concerns. It is just that simple to respond and just that simple to eat a bite of the humble pie and call it lesson learned. I have learned from that mistake and share it with others so no one else in the network has to make the same mistake that I made.

Since we have adapted to using e-mail/text messaging as a communication tools, we have to use this medium to translate non-verbal communication into verbal communication so the intended message can be encoded and decoded correctly. For marketing is communication and communication is marketing.

Quote #18 "Don't try to make people respect your reasoning, just give them no choice but to respect your results." - by Sulaiman Rahman

Islam, like Judaism and like Christianity is supposed to be, a religion of practice. It is not enough to know the religious rules and judgments but we are all required to practice what is preached. Submission to the will of Allah means I put my personal preferences aside for the greater good of mankind and striving for the reward of paradise. My mentor said "Don't try to make people respect your reasoning, just give them no choice but to respect your results." I embraced Islam with all the rules and the discipline because I wanted to be a better person on the righteous path. The result I am striving for is raising my children with a religious guide so when I am not available, they know how to make the right choice and pass a test in life. One of the major problems in today's society is that we focus so much on academic learning that we forgot moral values and soft "communication" skills that have a positive impact on self-esteem. When people don't care about themselves how can they possibly care about anyone else including their own families? These statistics become profound when we witness the nonchalant attitudes about the murders, the thefts, the rapes of our women, etc. that occur every day in our communities. That is why moral values need to e encouraged in our youth.

After 3+ years since I embraced the religion of Islam with the proper belief in one God and the last of the messengers, Prophet Muhammad sallallahu ^alayi wa sallam , I can see I am more focused, happier and at peace with life and my upcoming death. I am at peace with life while admittedly working on a personal development improvement plan because I see that I am not working alone. Our time on this earth is part of a continuing spectrum of people, some past, some present and some in the future, working to change the pendulum of economic empowerment for the majority of Philadelphians.

W. L. Shirer said "Most true happiness comes from one's inner life, from the disposition of the mind and soul. Admittedly, a good inner life is difficult to achieve, especially in these trying times. It takes reflection and contemplation and ...self-discipline." H. A. Dorfman said "Self-discipline is a form of freedom. It is freedom from laziness, lethargy, freedom from the expectations and demands, freedom from weakness, fear—and doubt. Self-discipline allows a person to feel his inner strength, his talent. He is master of, rather than a slave to, his thoughts and emotions."

Having self-discipline to stay away from things that harm oneself or in my case the haram (prohibited) matters allows me to focus on my inner strength to do the work necessary to achieve results defined in the personal development improvement plan.

I see business deals are much more successful when there is

a third party involved then when I try "to get out of the way" and allow business to be conducted between the two parties. Results good or bad must be measured in other words, accounted for and a person is held accountable. This information was critical to moving to the next step of an action plan. The plan of action means I have to work on my own "soft" communication skills and help our clients navigate the communication hurdles for a better community so the results can speak for themselves In sha Allah

Quote #19 "The only constant is change, and changes constantly." - by Marcus G. Williams III

I say "It really doesn't matter if you look at events as lessons or blessings." Many people are resistant to change. Those are people who have gotten comfortable. Those are people who accept the status quo. The status quo says more than 50% of Philadelphia Public School students will not graduate high school. The status quo says my son has a 1 and 3 chance of going to jail. Since I am a mother of 2 sons, my family has a 66% chance of seeing jail time. The status quo says 60% of young adults between the ages of 16 and 24 are unemployed. The International Business Times writes "According to data from its own police department, Philadelphia has the highest murder rate of the nation's ten largest cities – by a wide margin. In 2011, on a per-capita basis, Philadelphia recorded 20.7 homicides per 100,000 inhabitants. The next bloodiest city, Chicago, came in at 15.7, followed by Dallas at 10.9. In contrast, the murder rates in New York City is 6.1, and 7.8 in Los Angeles." Exactly why should I accept, be comfortable, not work to change these horrific statistics? My question, unfortunately, is why do I feel like I am in the minority for change. Change doesn't always have to be bad, it can be a good thing.

There was a mob scene to save Philadelphia Public Schools.

These were schools that were failing our future and directly feeding the prison system. To my chagrin, there were people wanting to save these so called "institutions of learning" that were failing in their singular mission of education (or completing their other secret mission of the mis-education) of their students.

We are living in the fastest rate of change known to man so far. The rate of information consumed in our grandparents lifetime is sent to our generation in 1 year. In the last 40 years, cars have become electric, hot water heaters obsolete, computers ubiquitous, cell phones for everyone, microwaves cook our food, houses are using heat that comes directly from the sun (solar energy), we touch screens instead of keyboards, we play our music on mp3's, we save our lives with smoke detectors, we know who the baby's daddy is with DNA testing, we receive our money from automated teller (atm) machines and the list goes on and on. How dare we think change should not happen.

As an Information Technology Professional, I was expected to learn and adapt to new technologies. I started coding in middle school using the BASIC programming language and wrote FORTRAN programs in high school. While in college we coded using Access SQL, COBOL and C++. I graduated just as the internet was starting to explode. We went from the client server distribution model to internet distribution model in what seemed like overnight.

That is why I find this quote "the only constant is change, and changes constantly" so profound. The world is constantly changing. The winning advantage for small business is flexibility to adapt to a changing environment quicker than big businesses. So, if business owners are resistant to change, they give up the strategic advantage of being able to quickly adapt.

When Michael Jackson passed I had to give my children a whole lesson on who he was and his impact on the world. They had no idea just like they have not had a home phone number and a pay phone looks like a relic. The next generation does not expect to work at a job for 40 years, they expect change. This is a time when the younger generation has a technological advantage that is practically untapped. As far as marketing is concern, business owners should outsource to the teenagers to update Instagram, Facebook, twitter and foursquare! At the age of 10 my daughter could send my clients invoices using Freshbooks!

They say human nature rejects change but the next generation is growing up in a constantly changing world. The religion of Islam says we should be learning from the cradle to the grave.

Isn't a benefit of acquiring knowledge is to change our behaviors? I have found that people will try to avoid changing jobs or changing status until the pain of the current situation becomes unbearable or their desires for something else are stronger than their fears. FEAR in their minds is real. Charles Stanley said "Fear stifles our thinking and actions. It makes indecisiveness that results in stagnation. I have known talented people who procrastinate indefinitely rather than risk failure. Lost opportunities cause erosion of confidence, and the downward spiral begins." Knowing that I play a small insignificant role in the Creators plan helps me tame fear and focus harder on the opportunities and blessings presented. I can't wait to change into the new and improved version of me. For the sake of our children and my business, we need to change!

Quote #20 "Everyone has a deadline, they just don't know what it is." - by Tara Colquitt

Rita Mae Brown said "A deadline is negative inspiration. Still, it is better than no inspiration at all." Deadline make me get the things I don't want to do done. I love my business but not everything I have to do in the business. Like most people, I tend to procrastinate with the things I don't like to do and the deadline is the driving force to getting it done.

Melanie Pinola wrote on lifehacker.com saying[16], "Deadlines are stressful for most of us, and yet they do serve their purpose as a force of action. Without them, who knows how many great products, works of art, and plain old everyday projects wouldn't exist." "The ultimate inspiration is the deadline" is a quote from Nolan Bushnell, inventor of Pong, and founder of Atari and the Chuck E. Cheese chain of restaurants. I loathe deadlines, but this quote makes me appreciate them a little bit more and reminds me to set a deadline for all the things I really want to get done. As Duke Ellington said, "Without a deadline, baby, I wouldn't do nothing."

Diana Scharf Hunt said "Goals are dreams with deadlines." We do not have an infinite amount of time. Which is why time is more important than money. As my children are growing up, I am reminded of the short time I have to spend influencing their lives and their decision making skills. H. Jackson Brown, Jr. wrote in his book called "Life's Little Instruction Book", "Don't say you don't have enough time. You have exactly the same number of hours per day that were given to Helen Keller, Pasteur, Michelangelo, Mother Teresa, Leonardo da Vinci, Thomas Jefferson, and Albert Einstein." When something is important, a person will make time for it. Most people make time to go to work to pursue financial goals so it becomes a priority, then they have less time to spend being a parent of positive influence.

Because I was aware of the fact that my health conditions can lead to early death in my thirties, I took the opportunity to re-evaluate my priorities. In the American financial system, money grows in value with time but I have known for quite a while that my health conditions leave me with no time to spare. As I discussed this with my accountability partner, she said "Everyone has a deadline, they just don't know what it is." Would we do the same thing we are doing today if we knew for certain our time was up tomorrow? In that regard I am fortunate to be conscious that my time is about to be up. When I embraced Islam three years ago, I really had to re-evaluate how I managed the most precious resource of time for the righteous path. How does one serve Allah, then serve the family and finally serve work? Those priorities were aligned with my intrinsic value system Alhamdulillah.

This is how I do it. I ask myself every day, if I were to die tomorrow would I be doing the same thing with my time today? If I can answer that question with performing my obligations and avoiding the sins (to serve Allah), being able to spend time with my children in the afternoons (to serve my family) and helping my clients to go the next level (serve work), then it was a good day and I can lay down satisfied. Writing my story allows my impact to outlive my life and that is why it became a priority with a 30 day deadline. You can tell what a person values by how they spend their time.

Friedrich Wilhelm Nietzsche said "Many are stubborn in pursuit of the path they have chosen, few in pursuit of the goal." The path I had chosen for business ownership to have time freedom was like a maze full of twists, turns, roadblocks and brick walls. It took me years, money, prayer, love of Allah and lots of people to get to the goal of time freedom. Basically, I work to buy time to serve Allah t'ala and spend time with my children. This time right here is the most valuable because as a role model, it is my job to shape how they make decisions. I will end this one with the same question I ask of myself, "If you knew you were going to die tomorrow, is this the way you would like to spend your last day?"

Quote #21 "Success is belief in yourself, belief in your product and belief in the system." - by My mentor, Sulaiman Rahman

My job is to help businesses grow by showing them how to move from people-dependent (where there is a person for a job) to systems dependent (where there is a system for a job). Becoming systems dependent allows companies to scale growth and generate employment opportunities. To fully embrace the concept you must believe that, "the system is greater than the knowledge of one single person." In toxic environments, people hold on to the job by sabotaging their co-workers or their relationship with a man by having a child. Relationships rot because they say "it is cheaper to keep her" (in a job or a relationship). That is why you must have belief that the system is greater than the knowledge of one single person. #believeitornot

Quote #22 "It is not what you know (because that is why you went into business), it is what you don't know that makes it too much." - by My accountability partner, Tara Colquitt

"All things being equal, people will do business with, and refer business to, those people they know, like and trust." by Bob Burg, author of Endless Referrals

My business journey was longer than most because I was just a tab bit hard headed. My mentor was very patient with me and let me move along at a snails' pace. I believed he worked with me for so long, two plus years, because I was consistent. I came to mostly every presentation on Monday nights and attended all the Tuesday night trainings which I thoroughly enjoyed, actively participated in Sunday's weekly phone teams, the quarterly Super Saturday's and the yearly conventions. How did I do all this? I had a network of sister girlfriends who supported my family and allowed me to work for US. Whatever accomplishments I have received have been a result of TEAM effort Alhamdulillah (All praises be to Allah).

My grandfather owned a landscaping business on the main line and my mother learned to cook from her ex-mother in law and ran a catering/baking business all throughout my teenage years. One summer she left her job to start a women's exercise apparel clothing line. During that summer I worked at Wendy's and what little money I had, I gave it to my mom to fuel her dreams. The business did not last very long but it provided me with inspiration at the impressionable age of 15.

My mentor told me when we first started working together that I needed an accountability partner but I did not listen. We were just starting to work together and in the beginning I did not disclose a lot of information to him mainly because of how much I respected him. A few years later, I was blessed with an accountability partner, Tara Colquitt, The Credit Woman, who worked early in the mornings also and we have been partners holding each other accountable for at least 4 years now.

During one of our early morning conversations, we were both overwhelmed with work. She said "It is not what you know (because that is why you went into business), it is what you don't know that makes it too much." What she meant was that we both had the skills to get the job, credit or technology, done but business is so much bigger than that. Business is not just providing a product or services and getting paid. There is the licensing and incorporating process of making a legal entity, the banking relationship, the financing structures, the marketing of finding a customer, the sales of getting the customer to purchase the product or service, the accounting and taxes at the city, state and federal level, the minority certification process, the continuous learning cycle, the networking events, the customer service to get repeat business and starting the process all over again with the next customer.

Quote #23 "Gratitude is like a currency. Many debts have been satisfied by a sincere gesture of it." #satisfyalldebts - My mentors, Sulaiman & Celia Rahman

The website tinybuddha.com gives these easy examples on how to show gratitude[30]:

Show Gratitude to People Who Love You

1. Share a specific example of something they did for you and how it made a difference in your life.

2. Do something little but thoughtful for them—like clean up after a big Sunday dinner!

3. Give a long, intimate hug; or if you know they don't like hugs, stick out your hand for a handshake to cater to their preferences *and* make them smile.

4. Tell them you're there if they have anything they want to talk about—and let them know they have your full attention.

5. Give them something of yours that you think they would enjoy, and let them know specifically why you want them to have it.

6. Invite them to do something you know they've always wanted to do.

7. Encourage them to try something you know they want

to try, but haven't yet because they're scared.

8. Offer to do something you know they don't enjoy doing, like organizing their closet or mowing their lawn.

9. Compliment them on a talent, skill, or strength that you admire.

10. Look them straight in the eyes and say, "You make the world a better place."

Show Gratitude to People Who Challenge You

11. Fully listen to what they have to say, instead of forming your rebuttal in your head and waiting to speak.

12. Thank them for introducing you to a new way to look at things, even if you still don't agree.

13. Pinpoint something you admire about their commitment to their beliefs—even if you don't hold them, as well.

14. Resist the urge to tell them they're wrong.

15. Challenge them right back to be the best they can be, with love and positive intentions.

16. If they inspired you to push outside your comfort zone, thank them for inspiring you to take a risk, and let them know how it paid off.

17. Write a blog post about how they helped you see

things differently and dedicate it to them.

18. Use the lesson this person teaches you through your interactions, whether it is patience, compassion, or courage.

19. Introduce them to someone who may challenge them and help them grow, as they've done for you.

20. Let them know how you appreciate when they challenge you in a loving, non-confrontational way—and if they don't do that, be calm and kind when you ask them to do that going forward.

Show Gratitude to People Who Serve You

21. Give a larger tip than usual.

22. If they have a tip jar, include a thoughtful note of appreciation along with your coins or bills.

23. Smile when you order or enlist their assistance. Smiles are contagious, so give one away!

24. If they serve you regularly, acknowledge something they always do well—like work efficiently or stay calm under pressure.

25. Exhibit patience, even if you're in a hurry.

26. Let their superior know they do an outstanding job.

27. Keep their workplace clean—for example, at a coffee shop, clean up after yourself at the sugar stand.

28. Offer to get a coffee for them, if it is someone working in or outside your home.

29. If you have their contact information, send an email of appreciation—and let them know you just wanted to express your gratitude, so they don't need to write back.

30. Praise them in a review on Yelp and/or recommend them to people you know.

Show Gratitude to People Who Work with You

31. Write a handwritten thank you note, acknowledging things you value about them and their work.

32. Offer to lighten their workload in some way if you are able.

33. Bring back lunch for them if you know they're working hard and likely haven't had a chance to grab something.

34. If you're running a meeting, keep it short to show them you appreciate and respect their time.

35. Ask them about their lives instead of always being all business. This doesn't mean you need to pry into personal matters; it just means showing an interest in who they are as people.

36. Be the calm, light voice in a stressful situation.

37. Give them flowers to brighten their desk.

38. Let their boss know how they're doing a great job and contributing to the company.

39. Listen fully if they're having a difficult day, and recognize if they need space to figure things out on their own, not advice or help.

40. Remember the little things can make a big difference!

Show Gratitude for Yourself

41. Make a list of ways you've impressed yourself lately.

42. Treat yourself to something you enjoy.

43. If someone compliments you, thank them.

 44. Compliment yourself.

45. Give yourself time to enjoy a passion you're sometimes too busy to fit in.

46. Take an inventory of all the good things you've done for other people and the world.

47. Write yourself a love letter.

48. Let go of any conditions you have for being kind to yourself—meaning you appreciate even if you didn't accomplish or do anything specific.

49. Schedule a date with yourself—an afternoon or evening that's all about you.

50. Share the beauty that is you with the people around you, knowing they're fortunate to have you in their lives.

Show Gratitude for Your Clients

51. Get their work done – AHEAD OF SCHEDULE.

52. Be ON TIME.

53. Open when you say your business is open.

54. Keep the area and neighborhood tidy.

55. Offer reward or loyalty cards.

56. Do something nice for a random customer.

57. Say THANK YOU.

58. Send your client a handwritten thank you card.

59. SHOW UP!

The difference I see in living in Philadelphia compared to living in Washington DC is gratitude. Let's not get this twisted because gratitude like in my case, obesity, is just a symptom of the problem. People who don't love themselves can't be grateful for anything because they have no appreciation of self. That brings us to the real issue and that issue is self-esteem. We all know, there are lids in life. We call them glass ceilings, crabs in a barrel and all other type of names. The lid on love is self-esteem. It is impossible for a person to appreciate another who does not appreciate him/herself.

Quite simply, I see many African-American men who do not appreciate women outside of the bedroom. It is very sad, that I also see many African-American women who don't appreciate themselves outside of the bedroom too. As my consultant and I talk about this issue, we noticed that relationships are based on physical attraction. Is there anything else? I hear guys say about their current wife (or soon to be ex-wife) "When I am done with her..." or what I recently heard "I had to let her go", etc... That is the current cycle of self-destruction that has ripped through the African-American community. We feed our boys into the education then to the prison pipeline and accept substandard treatment by women and men who lack self-esteem. African-American men are not grateful to the mothers that bore them or the wife who attended to their needs and in most cases desires. Somehow we have to get back to teaching our boys to open doors for women, take the trash out, and carry the bags so they know how to treat women like queens and receive treatment from that same woman as a king.

It takes more than acts of gratitude to treat the self-esteem problem. But like the quote says "many debts have been satisfied by a sincere gesture of it" we have to start somewhere and begin to raise the lid.

Quote #24 "Labels are for products not people. Don't let people put labels on you when they don't know what you're made of." - by Camari Ellis

The Kid Counselor wrote in an article[17], "We live in a society that labels everything. We have labels on our clothes, our cheeseburgers, our meat and produce, and the list goes on. We like the convenience of neatly packaged words so we can sum up the person, place or thing and know what to expect. However, especially with children, even harmless labels can play a lasting role in self-esteem, behavior and long-term personality."

Children develop and define their sense of self by processing what others tell them about who they are, what they are good at, how they behave and so on. The communication principle of the "Looking-Glass Self" from Charles Cooley can be applied. Cooley believes that "by reflecting back to us who we are and how we come across, other people function as mirrors for us.

Imagine the implication then, for children, when we 'reflect' on who they are. Every time a teacher says he or she is a "good student" or a coach says "average player," that helps define the way the child views him or herself. If you notice one child pursues musical interests, he becomes "the musician." Another loves sports, and she becomes "the athlete." Another excels in school and is the "brainiac." None of those labels have negative connotations, but can pigeonhole children into pre-defined boxes. What if the "brainiac" really wants to try soccer? Unfortunately, there is already an "athlete" in the family, which builds a fight or flight response. She can either fight to redefine her place as a smart child who also plays soccer, or can revert back to the place where she has already been.

Labels have much more of an impact than we realize, and we need to be mindful of how we talk about our children. If you must define certain things about them to yourself or others, try to choose positive versions of the same trait, i.e. "spirited" rather than "hyper," "cautious" instead of "timid." Being mindful of the descriptions we give off to children can make a difference in the self-esteem and self-concept that they develop. The self-fulfilling prophecy can go both ways - a child told he is lazy will likely be so, but the opposite is also true that a child told they are helpful will help. Keeping the focus on the child's positive attributes, while avoiding labels, can encourage children (and adults) to become healthy and happy."

These labels do not stop at youth but they are carried into adulthood because the child took the label into their person. As a child, my mother refused to let anyone label me in a negative way. I never thought of myself as fat. I was just big like everyone else in my family. I was always labeled smart and even some considered me "pretty" but this was one label I could not accept. I had and still have a problem with that because if I was judged pretty, did we judge others are ugly?

I personally refused to be label by constantly learning which keeps me in state of becoming as opposed to a state of BE. My motto is "Stop trying to fit in when you were born to stand out." Each of us took a different journey into this moment. It is the unique experience that brings a new perspective - YOU ARE DIFFERENT FROM EVERYONE ELSE so act like it! One technique to avoid is comparison to other people. This helps to recognize our unique blessings. I hear people all the time compare themselves to others - IT IS TO BE AVOIDED. I was asked the following questions for an interview 1) What differences do you observe between you and other mainstream women entrepreneurs? 2) What similarities do you observe between you and other mainstream women entrepreneurs? My answer to both questions was , I don't have time to compare. When you are truly focused on your goals, what others do, say or have is of no consequence to you and your mission. That is why I truly agree with the quote "Labels are for products not people. Don't let people put labels on you when they don't know what you're made of."

Quote #25 "When everything is going wrong, that's when you know you are on the right path. Good things come to those who wait." – by My mentor, Sulaiman Rahman

My mentor who is 4 years younger than me, shared "When everything is going wrong, that's when you know you are on the right path. Good things come to those who wait." I will add -- with good intentions. Words of wisdom from a wise young man!

Quote #26 "You are only a true entrepreneur if you only make money from your efforts." – My accountability partner, Tara Colquitt

When a person declares they are an entrepreneur, the first question that usually asked is "how long have you been in business?" That question usually tells the person if they are any good at their business. The next question is usually "are you doing this full time or part time?" As a good friend of mine said "A slave cannot serve two masters." Many people think they are business owners, with a product or service, business card and a website if their income is not solely dependent on their business, then they still answer to what pays them income and that is their job. Their business is just a nice paying hobby and by Tara Colquitt's definition, that person is not truly an entrepreneur.

An entrepreneur is a person who organizes and operates a business or businesses, taking on greater than normal financial risks in order to do so. What I have learned is that entrepreneurs come in every shape and size and not everyone is serious about their business. Most people who claim they are business owners really have nice hobbies. That is why the government had to make a distinction between a hobby and a business. The IRS website says[1], "Is your hobby really an activity engaged in for profit?

In general, taxpayers may deduct ordinary and necessary

expenses for conducting a trade or business or for the production of income. Trade or business activities and activities engaged in for the production of income are activities engaged in for profit.

The following factors, although not all inclusive, may help you to determine whether your activity is an activity engaged in for profit or a hobby:

- Does the time and effort put into the activity indicate an intention to make a profit?
- Do you depend on income from the activity?
- If there are losses, are they due to circumstances beyond your control or did they occur in the start-up phase of the business?
- Have you changed methods of operation to improve profitability?
- Do you have the knowledge needed to carry on the activity as a successful business?
- Have you made a profit in similar activities in the past?
- Does the activity make a profit in some years?
- Do you expect to make a profit in the future from the appreciation of assets used in the activity?

An activity is presumed for profit if it makes a profit in at least three of the last five tax years, including the current year (or at least two of the last seven years for activities that consist primarily of breeding, showing, training or racing horses).

If an activity is not for profit, losses from that activity may not be used to offset other income. An activity produces a loss when related expenses exceed income. The limit on not-for-profit losses applies to individuals, partnerships, estates, trusts, and S corporations. It does not apply to corporations other than S corporations."

On our daily accountability call, my partner said, "For every twelve people who say they are business owners there is just 1 real owner." I would add, the rest are just hustling. In this context, hustle means[2] "An illicit or unethical way of doing business or obtaining money; a fraud or deceit." My mentor said to me years ago "Treat it like a business and it will pay you like a business."

On the first meeting with a potential client, I usually ask "what are your goals?" Typically, the answer is "hmm, let me think." The second question, "what is the break-even number (i.e.) how much does it cost to run the business monthly?" Typically the answer is less than $1,000. My follow up question is "does that include paying yourself?" The answer is "no." Those three questions tell me the person is treating their business as a hustle (i.e. a hobby) and they are not a true entrepreneur. When the business is treated like a business, the goals include paying all expenses, paying the owner(s) AND making a profit! The profit is then used to hire resources (i.e. employees, contractors, etc.) so the business owner(s) enjoys time freedom.

I tell business owners all the time, my first mistake was hiring an accountant. As I continue to deal with incompetent accountants, I realize my mistake. When true entrepreneurs are serious about their business, they can only do business with people who are also serious about their business. NEVER trust the business to those who have a JOB. I also advise clients to avoid business advice from those with a job for the same reason. Doing good work for the business is not their priority.

I know many business owners who started their business while working but the intention for business owners is to get paid for doing what they love and not trying to make "extra" income. Hustlers are looking to make extra money who have proven that they are not willing to "treat it as a business with an accounting system, employees, overhead (i.e. office expense) to allow the "business to pay the owner as a business." In the long run, they are selling themselves short. That is why hustlers can't keep clientele because if the business owner is "selling themselves short," they will most likely "sell the customer short too."

True entrepreneurs beware and put the necessary systems in place to separate your business from the hustlers.

Quote #28 "Everything you want is on the other side of FEAR #getoverit." – My mentor, Sulaiman Rahman

Lessons Learned From Mentors

My partner said "Everything you want is on the other side of FEAR. Get over it" and I said to my client "Never fear, your network is here." #nolimits

Quote #28 "Giving people self-confidence is by far the most important thing that I can do. Because then they will ACT." - by Jack Welch

Most of the changes implemented in my business have been the result of another change which I could not control. Two years ago I was forced to change e-mail marketing provider when iContact decided to stop paying for referrals to their existing clients. This year, I am moving banks because my credit union that I have been with for almost 20 years started charging to have a business checking account. Tara Colquitt and I implemented the Calling All Female Entrepreneurs (C.A.F.E) series after losing our ability to talk to potential clients at the monthly orientation with our largest sponsor. Changes are bound to happen but what is important is the reaction to change. That's when the real test begins. Think of the change as negative, then it is more likely to have a negative impact. Think of the change as positive, then it is more likely to have a positive impact. Not all changes are for the worst. Becoming a business owner can be a very scary feeling. In essence, people are breaking from the norms of society and taking a risk that they have something to offer and can put a price on their offering. My mentor summed up the fear and risk quite nicely by saying "Everything you want is on the other side of FEAR #getoverit." Getting over it is, of course, easier said than done. The Calling All Female Entrepreneurs series was designed to push women who are sitting on the ledge of a choice. The choice is to jump off and sink or learn how to fly while falling. It might be said, that it is the "do or die" decision. I know what it feels like because that's what my mentor did for me. He pushed me over the edge but gave me the confidence to fly while I was falling. I used to tell him that I was trying and like yoda said in Star Trek "Do or do not. There is no try." That's where self-confidence comes into play. What I sell to business owners is self-confidence with a series of homework assignments. The process is that my company and our network can help them grow their business using technology tools so their business can be run efficiently. I sell what my mentor gave me for practically free. The Tuesday night training sessions were only 10 dollars and over 2 years that was great investment of only $1,040 dollars.

Making the decision to do, not try is half the battle but business is not about one person. Business Dictionary defines business as "an organization or economic system where goods and services are exchanged for one another or for money." Every business requires some form of investment and enough customers to whom its output can be sold on a consistent basis in order to make a profit. Business owners by their very nature need to be leaders. The success of their business is dependent on what other people (customers, suppliers, employees, strategic partners, etc.) are willing to do. Business owners have to make decisions. Do they want to be managers or leaders? Peter Drucker defined management and leadership as "Management is doing things right; leadership is doing the right things." Dr. Stephen R. Covey further stated "Leadership is a choice, not a position." So, a business owner can manage a process that is inefficient and has a negative impact on the bottom line or become a leader that uses their own self-confidence to change the process to do the right things which positively impact the bottom line.

Self-confidence is the key to motivate people into action! Generally, the more people achieve, the more self-confident they become. So the building blocks of self-confidence did not begin with making a decision to own a business. They began in childhood as people had to keep falling but trying again to learn how to walk. The keys to self confidence began as people started bringing home report cards and getting signs of approval from their families. The keys to self-confidence became achievement blocks to completing high school, college, etc. That is where we as a people have failed. Learning does not stop at high school or college or in a formal environment. Learning and being receptive to learn has to continue throughout an entire lifetime. We are not supposed to become adults and just accept our lot in life. We all know that change is bound to happen to continue to sharpen the skill set in preparation for the next challenge.

That is why business owners need to be leaders. Leaders develop skill sets in other people. Why do this? Because the development of skill sets in others benefits the bottom line of the business. In a few of our Tuesday night trainings, we talked about the leadership lid. A business can never go beyond the lid of the leader. John Maxwell posted on his blog[15], "Leadership Ability Determines a Person's Level of Effectiveness - leadership ability is the lid that determines a person's level of effectiveness. The lower an individual's ability to lead, the lower the lid on his potential. The higher the individual's ability to lead, the higher the lid on his potential. To give you an example, if your leadership rates an 8, then your effectiveness can never be greater than a 7. If your leadership is only a 4, then your effectiveness will be no higher than a 3. Your leadership ability—for better or for worse—always determines your effectiveness and the potential impact of your organization." So when leaders continue to develop their own potential (increasing the lid) while using a set of assignments that provide self-confidence to the people surrounding them, that is a business that is moving on one accord at the highest levels of action. I have seen it done on a small firm and I saw it done at a firm with 135,000 employees worldwide. This is called #vision.

Quote #29 "If you are your authentic self, you have no competition." - by Author Unknown

They say "One of the greatest challenges in life is being yourself in a world that is trying to make you like everyone else." One of the first requirements of business is looking at our competitors. The business owner has to know there is a need in the market that is not being met by the competition. This goes against what was instilled in me by my mother. She showed me that I am unique with a purpose driven mission and a duty to fulfill. That does not mean I am perfect. Like everyone else, I have many, many flaws. Zig Ziglar said "Until you are happy with who you are, you cannot be happy with what you have." Which is why people who receive a lot of money at one time, always go back to where they were before. Rob Liano said "A person will never attain and maintain more than they think they deserve." Their financial wealth cannot go beyond how they feel inside.

This is a story I posted on Facebook a few years ago. Recently, I had the pleasure of enjoying company with my children, my neighbor's children and my daughter's BFF on our walk to the library and the playground. My daughters BFF asked me, "Why are you smiling?" I said "because I am happy." She said "You're always happy..." That's my job because when mommy is happy, my children are happy. Just like when mommy is sad, depressed, angry -- my children are sad, depressed and angry. Lesson learned make sure your circle of influence is HAPPY.

A person has to make an internal decision (choice) on how they want to live their life. We all have outside influences that affect our decisions. I was influenced by my mentor to become a better person and I was influenced by one of my BFF's to choose the righteous path of Islam. Those were positive influences. I am blessed because I was surrounded by mostly positive influences unlike many other people. My mentor said "Don't let other people's BS (Belief System) affect YOU (Your Own Understanding) and keep you broke and miserable!" People who are unhappy try to influence other people to join them in their misery. They say "misery loves company."

So, how does one become their authentic self while being constantly told to "get ahead of the competition" or to join a circle of negative influences? The first thing is to realize that everyone does not have a person's best interest at heart. If they do not want another person to improve, it is because the person does not want to improve their self. There are many people satisfied with the status quo.

When negative people are removed from the circle of influence, in most cases, they are replaced by positive people. They say "Everyone is insane, you just want them to be self-aware of their own insanity." Nobody is perfect. Relationships (friend, marriage, business, etc.) must accept imperfections and COMMUNICATE them as areas of self-improvement.

Every relationship should strive to make a person better. This is definitely a challenge. Most people are not very good communicators. Communication is not just saying anything. It requires talking and they say "talk is cheap." Communication is conveying a message so that is it received as it is intended. It not only has to be said in a positive manner but it also must be heard. I am still learning how to do this. That is why we are all a work in progress and learning continues from the "cradle to the grave."

Bruce Lee said "know your limits... AND SURPASS THEM." The quicker a person realizes they can't do it all, the better. Surpassing limits is growth. The human condition shows that we need each other to surpass our own limits. That is why they say "IRON sharpens IRON" and "TEAM work makes the DREAM work." People need people, like a student needs a teacher, to improve upon their own knowledge. The teacher remains a student of knowledge and the student of knowledge strives to be a teacher.

A person can get to their authentic self by utilizing the power of focus and the practice of discipline. H. A. Dorfman correctly said "Self-discipline is a form of freedom. It is freedom from laziness, lethargy, freedom from the expectations and demands, freedom from weakness, fear—and doubt. Self-discipline allows a person to feel his inner strength, his talent. He is master of, rather than a slave to, his thoughts and emotions." I am happy not only to get to the place of self-discipline but I have learned to be happy on the journey. The journey is becoming disciplined to find my authentic self.

#Quote #30 "Children learn more from who you are than what you teach." - by W.E.B. Du Bois

Lessons Learned From Moms:

For my children: Do not be fooled by the word independence. You were not born nor shall you be independent. You are alive by the will of God. Your actions are intended to please God by serving the community. This is our obligation. Your life will be blessed beyond measure with this understanding.

Lessons Learned From Moms:

My job as a mom is to make my children believe they are winners too, like my mother believed (no matter who told her I was not smart enough, thin enough, pretty enough, etc...) in ME!!!

A friend of mine just recently told me that I have women's liberation movement written all over me. I did not even know that. It is so subconscious in my mind that only when she said this to me did it become conscious. I am a product of the 70's Women's Liberation Movement. I must have traces of burning bras somewhere in my closet.

First, unless something is specifically said to me, I usually don't take the time to observe what other people do. I grew up with no gender roles as I saw my mother and my both my grandmother's playing mom and dad. There were no male figures in my immediate circle except my BFF's dad. I also had an unclear set of moral values. I was told that "I could be anything I wanted to be" and "the world was my oyster." It wasn't until I embraced Islam that I actually knew there were roles for women and for men. I was sure there were roles for men but the roles for women, I thought were actually for other women unlike me. Those roles were for domestic women and I wanted no part of that job!

Most of my friends' mom were also single moms and our society, in general, has wrongfully said it is okay and somewhat expected for women to have children without a man. When I had my first child at the ripe old age of 28 no one said anything to me about being an unwed mother except one person who was a female pastor and a good friend of my mothers. I did what I was told to do. I got the good grades, finished college, got a good paying job and owned my own home had 20,000 in the bank before I became a parent. My mom had told me to have a child for me and not for a man. So I did that too. I had my child for me and the man was not a consideration. I took the value system of my family to not get married but only have children with one person. I went on to have more children with this man so my children would have the same father.

Someone said to me "you are out of place." Did everyone else but me know that I had a place? My family grew up in the

Baptist church as a result I was left to "explore" my own religion. At that time, I chose non-belief in anything. In my own ignorance of moral/religious values, marriage was not even a consideration. I was the one who left my children's father in Washington D.C. to move to Philadelphia. I am a realist and marriage requires work that, at the time, I was unwilling to commit myself to doing. This is what happens when parents are not willing to be the example of what they want them to learn. Marriage is for my own protection but I did not even know that because there were not enough women role models showing that to me.

So, if I want my children to do something different, I have to show them different. I wanted my children to grow up with a clear set of moral/religious values not the American values. The American value system centers around what is popular and who is the president-elect. For example, it is acceptable by American standards and prohibited by the religious standards of Islam to be gay or lesbian. The American values are subject to change with the wind. The moral/religious value system guides a person to what is lawful (halal) and what is unlawful (haram). Teaching my children through words is not enough. That is why they say "children learn more from what you show them than what you teach." It has to be reinforced through the daily habits of discipline and the practice of the value system. Even then it is hard because some Muslims wish to remain ignorant or not practice what has been prescribed to them.

In The Early Birds Think Tank, yesterday's discussion was Individual vs. Group. Camari Ellis said "I always hear people speak with pride about how much of an individual they are. Rarely do I have people speak with pride about being a member of a group(ex. Fraternity/Sorority or Church). Is one more important than the other?" I responded "The TEAM heads down is more important. Michael Jordan hit the nail on the nose with "Individuals win games but teamwork and intelligence win championships." First, I don't like black for the sake of black. Barack Obama would not be the president if he depended on black folk. When the agenda is about what is good for everyone then WE all win. I focus on buying black as a benefit for non-blacks too." Camari Ellis□ then said "Maybe it is me, but I don't think most see it that way." I said, "That is why we have a crisis in the black community. Too many of US have individual goals and do not have enough family teams properly structured. In the family team, the needs of many children outweigh the needs of a few or one. That is what needs to be fixed for an economic and social unified community. And as all of you should know by now I am speaking about myself." I have to step up and be the solution to my own problem. I would talk some more but it is dinner time. Someone has to be the example teaching my daughter to cook and teaching my sons to clean.

Quote #31 "Success isn't measured by money or power or social rank. Success is measured by your discipline and inner peace." - by football coach and legend, Mike Ditka

Arnold H Glassow said, "Success isn't a result of spontaneous combustion. You must set yourself on fire." From my experience, I know now that I was set up to be successful. First, we have to define the terms for an effective conversation. Mike Ditka, the football coach and legend said "Success isn't measured by money or power or social rank. Success is measured by your discipline and inner peace." I define success as hitting a goal and successful is having the mindset that success is possible. My mother loved me. She might not have always liked me but love is a verb and I was protected/loved fiercely by my mother. I was protected from the doctor's who told her I was overweight, from the people who tried in vain to tell me NO, and from having the POOR mindset that things were not possible for an African-American female from West Philadelphia. She was my advocate and my voice and she instilled confidence, not arrogance, in me. Like how I strive to show my children, I had choices and options from a young age.

When I was going to the 5th grade my choices were Masterman or Friends Select. Technically, we missed the deadline for the "special admission process" for Masterman but I learned from my mother that the decision maker does not sit in the big chair but the desk in front of the chair and that's how I got in. This year, I gave my daughter who was going into the 7th grade a choice on her school, TIES which is a private school or PA Leadership Charter School. She chose to go to TIES which makes it her choice to not only do well but exceed in her education and religious endeavors.

Just like I know that I was set up to be successful, I know that many other people have been and are being set up for failure. New America Media reports[19], "A coalition of African-Americans educators say the nation's public school system is giving up on black male students and setting them up to fail. According to "Yes We Can: The 2010 Schott 50 State Report on Black Males in Public Education," the overall 2007-2008 graduation rate for black males in the U.S. was only 47 percent, and half of the states have graduation rates for black male students below the national average. The report highlights concerns that New York's graduation rate for its Regents diploma is only 25 percent for black male students. New York City, the district with the nation's highest enrollment of black students, only graduates 28 percent of its black males with Regents diplomas on time. Overall, each year, more than 100,000 black male students in New York City do not graduate from high school. Without targeted investments to provide the core, research-proven resources to help black male students succeed in public education," the report concludes, they are being set up to fail."

The fourth report released by the Schott Foundation for Public Education provides state-by-state data that shows which U.S. school districts and states are failing to provide the resources black male students need for the opportunity to learn. "These boys are failing, but I believe that it is the responsibility of the adults around them to turn these trajectories around," Geoffrey Canada, President and CEO of the Harlem Children's Zone, said in a statement. "All of us must ensure that we level the playing field for the hundreds of thousands of children who are at risk of continuing the cycle of generational poverty. The key to success is education."

This report clearly specifies the problem and the solution. As a mother of two African-American males it is my responsibility like my mother showed me to place them in an "environment of success." So, if I know the public schools will not allow them to thrive, if I know the private schools see them as just money then I have to place them somewhere else where they are loved (love is a verb) and given the tools to be successful. The United States has given up on the outdated public school system and putting the responsibility back on to the parents shoulders. I am happy to report that my boys are on the honor roll this year and that is what gives them confidence to be successful in any endeavor they chose to accomplish.

Dodinsky said "You can find inspiration from others but determination is solely your responsibility." Determination is having the will to move from thoughts to action for the pursuit of a goal. Determination is "setting yourself on fire."

Remember what Glasow said "Success isn't a result of spontaneous combustion. You must set yourself on fire."

Quote #32 "How you do anything is how you do everything." - by Author Unknown. #notimeforgames #raisethebar

Lessons Learned From Mentors

Don't listen to naysayers. As an entrepreneur, plenty of people have tried to tell me what I can't do. I look and laugh because I know those people are saying what THEY can't do. #donotlisten #sethighexpectations

What we rarely see, however, are stories about the numerous companies that are managed by ethical leaders. While standards seem to keep falling in some corporations, other leaders "raise the bar" and inspire their teams to do the same. These leaders do the right thing, at the right time, and for the right reasons. They put their ethics before the bottom line – and as a result, they have dedicated teams that would do almost anything for them. So, how do they do it? And how can you do it as well? We'll show you how to define your own ethical standards – and start putting those standards into practice. Define Your Organization's Values. In order to lead your team with character and integrity, you must set an example. You're the leader, remember? Your team looks to you. To begin, you must know your own values as well as your organization's values.

Hopefully, your company has clear rules about how it wants team members to act. As a leader, it is up to you to know these rules and codes of conduct – and to make sure you enforce them. Your personal values are also important. If the company's written rules don't say that you must be fair to everyone, but this value is important to you – then, of course, you're going to do it. Good leaders follow their personal values as well as organizational values. Ask yourself these questions: What standards of behavior are really important to my company? What specific values do I admire in certain leaders? Do I identify with those values? Would I still live by those values, even if they put me at a competitive disadvantage? Set the tone now that you know your company's core values and build the right environment for your team and your organization. Again, leading by example is the best way to do this. It is what you do, not what you say, that demonstrates to your team what you care about. So, if your company values honesty above all else, then make sure you demonstrate that by being honest with everyone around you. If your company values free speech, then make sure you allow your team to communicate their ideas openly. Next, establish consequences for team members who don't follow corporate values. If you allow someone to come in late continuously without making up the hours, that won't set a good example for the rest of the team. You need good consequences as well. Set up some kind of reward system for team members who consistently act according to the company values. Storytelling is a great way to reinforce and communicate these values. If you know of team members or even clients who acted ethically in difficult situations, then tell their stories. This shows your staff that they can do it as well. By getting your team interested in ethical conduct, you communicate how important these values are to both you and your organization.

Quote #33 "No one can make you feel inferior without your consent." - by Eleanor Roosevelt

If the "green eye" of envy has overcome a person that means emotional self-discipline was not in place to fight the emotion of envy. Just like if someone says something negative about a person and that person reacts by being "hurt" that also means that emotional self-discipline was not strong enough to fight that emotion. Discipline is used in every area of our lives including the area of emotions. Even in this area, I have to use the rules of the religion of Islam to deal with emotions. I have become a giver after being tested with many trials that shook me to the core. I now recognize every day as a blessing. I have been blessed with many gifts by "wanting for my sister what I want for myself."

Here is my list of seven ways to stay emotionally strong so other people who try to make one feel inferior are not successful at their goal:

1. Live with an "Attitude of Gratitude" by learning to love yourself. A person can learn to love their self by practicing forgiveness. People can also learn to apologize and recognize saying sorry is not an admission of guilt. For me, an apology shows that I value the relationship and I am "grateful" for that person to be in my life. Showing love to other people is how one learns to love them self. When a person loves them self, they will find it much easier to stop doing the things that harm them. That is why people should not invest in people who don't love themselves. People who don't love themselves find it harder to stop harming themselves AND THOSE AROUND THEM.

2. Don't want too much. Psychology Today says[26], "Desire can be a powerful motivating tool, but wanting something too much can be very painful and very expensive, so don't live beyond your means or covet the unattainable. Seek your desire, but keep your integrity." Most people think having more money will solve all their problems. That is the picture painted on television. My mother would say "those people have problems too." When I was making the most money in my life I was the unhappiest. Our most precious asset is time not money. If I am using the day to practice the beauty of Islam and benefit my clients, then I feel good about the use of time. We have no time (not money) to waste.

3. Watch the company you keep. They say "hurt people, hurt people" and we are living in a time with many hurt people. Human communication, lack of communication and expectations make it very easy to start disagreements and misplaced feelings. Please consider the source. Most times it is the other person's issue so it can just be ignored. If the other person has no impact on a person's goals then it is so much easier to focus on beneficial relationships. Every relationship should make you better in some way. So people who hurt others, people who ask others to partake in sinful behavior are no good for inner peace and have to be removed one way or another from the area of focus. The only people who deserve to be in your life are those willing to pay for it. If they are not willing to build a proper, committed relationship that is respectful by both parties, move on.

4. Recognize that disappointment is part of life. My mom showed me that "failure was success in progress." Psychology Today wrote "Even the most successful people have to deal with disappointment, but they've learned how to use it to get to the next level of life." Failure is a success if the lesson learned can be applied. My mom would also say "Life will keep giving you the same card, until the reaction is different." So if a person is facing the same hurdle, they have to deal with it differently on the next go round.

5. Deal with fear. Remember, fears are all in our head. One of my mentors said, "Everything you want is on the other side of FEAR #getoverit." A few years ago, I went on a team building excursion with one of my former employers. We had to swing on a rope to get from one side of the bridge to the other. The bridge was literally 3 feet from the ground but I was so afraid it felt like I was jumping off a 30 story building WITH NO ROPE. I cried and cried in front of the whole team but eventually (or 30 minutes later) I was successful in overcoming that fear. They say "fear makes you stronger, and being a little scared can make you better. You want to have butterflies; you just want them flying in formation. It helps to understand and admit your fears. Then you can kick them to the curb." Getting over that fear helped me get over bigger tests in life.

6. Be friends with life by believing in a higher purpose. When a person understands that life is a test, it is easier to take a "long term view" of the situation. There is no need to react "in the heat of the moment." Take a moment to pray on it and be guided by higher power other than the negative thoughts that creep in our minds.

7. Keep negative thoughts at bay. That is helped by #1 "having an attitude of gratitude." Before a person can dwell on the negative situation, it could always become worse so they have to learn to be thankful for what they have. They say a key to "wealth is health." For me, the key to my happiness was submission to the will of Allah Alhamdulillah. I am thankful for being guided on the righteous path. It is hard to think positive all the time. I was taught to live each day as if it was my last. So if today is my last day, why would I waste a moment with negativity when I am surrounded by my children with a roof over our head and food in our stomachs?

Once a person has a life that is directed by love, they are able to give and receive love. That is what is needed so there is no consent when another person tries to make one feel inferior.

Quote #34 "Successful and unsuccessful people do not vary greatly in their abilities. They vary in their desires to reach their potential." by John Maxwell

First we have to define success. My definition of success has changed many times because success has been different as my goals have been different at each stage of my life. Like most children, I thought success was having a lot of money. GEOFFREY JAMES, the author correctly writes in his article[4], "If you believe success is simply making (or having) a lot of money, you may be setting yourself up for failure. It is very strange, because many of the people who think this way are harried, stressed and, frankly, pretty miserable. Even so, I'd rather be poor and happy than rich and miserable."

As I was able to overcome obstacles like getting accepted into the prestigious Masterman Middle School (thank you EEOC) and getting accepted into the High School of Engineering and Science (again thank you EEOC) and getting my first job to achieve goals, I noticed those were successful moments. But they were just moments of happiness brought on by overcoming an obstacle to achieve the desired goal.

I have learned through the school of hard knocks that my many failures were success in progress. Success now ties to happiness. So if I am successful, which is way different than having a successful moment then I am happy. They say,

"When mom is happy, the children are happy. When mom is unhappy, the children are unhappy." Examining my own life and others, I have found this to be true. So, now I have an obligation for the sake of my children to seek happiness which is success so they can be happy too!

What I find so very interesting is yes I am happy so I am successful but I crave the challenge. The greater the challenge, the greater the reward. Richard St. John's says in TEDTalks[27], "There are 8 secrets of success.

1) Have Passion

2) Have fun working

3) Get good at it - Practice, Practice, Practice

4) Focus on one thing

5) Push yourself through shyness and self-doubt. Let others push you (i.e. that's what Mothers are for)

6) Serve - Make it a point to server others something of value

7) Ideas - THINK

8) Have Persistence. You must be able to persist through failure."

See I told you failure was success in progress!

The fact that I am writing book #4 is amazing to me. I barely passed English in high school and had to take remedial writing courses in college. Out of the possible 800 points I could get on the English section of the SAT's, my score was a dismal 440 (and that was a 10% increase over the 400 I got the first time!). My mother is the writer in our family and I refused to show her a single paper until I was 25 years old when I applied for graduate school. I was embarrassed by my weak writing skills especially since my mother was a writer. Though I still don't write very well, I am better because I practiced with a blog, practiced writing 3 articles for Examiner and then practiced writing some more. They say "you get better with practice" so instead of accepting the failure (i.e. self doubt) just get up and practice some more. That is what Richard St. John meant by pushing yourself through self doubt.

I was attracted to Islam because of my belief in Allah and the last of the prophets, Prophet Muhammad sallallah ^alayi wa sallam (Peace be upon him). There are no shortcuts on the righteous path and it is about self-improvement. That sounds a lot like what John C. Maxwell said in his quote "Successful and unsuccessful people do not vary greatly in their abilities. They vary in their desires to reach their potential." Now the definition of success I use is the daily goal of serving my customers, serving my religion and striving on the path to paradise. Paraphrase that sentence into this quote: "success is the sum of small efforts, repeated day in and day out." That is the success I seek daily to allows my family and I to go to bed happy and plan for tomorrow's success.

I am just a slave striving on the righteous path. They say

"failure is success in progress" which means, I am on the right path to learn Arabic by being persistent and getting back up after each failed attempt to try again. Alhamdulillah :-0

Quote #35 "All business is personal." - by Barry Schwartz

In his Strictly Business Blog, Barry Schwartz said[28], "A great politician (they do exist)." Tip O'Neill, famously once said "All politics is local." There are a lot of ways to interpret that idea, but it starts with the fact that politics is about people. Business too is about people

Pretty much everyone in every business wants to work with people they like (and with work they like). They crave a human connection. Strategies to make that connection are endless and success can be excruciatingly arbitrary: sometimes you don't know who will click with whom (or what work will click) until the clicking is all over.

It is about matching sensibilities, or taste, or imagination, or maybe the phase of the moon. Whatever. A connection is a connection. Imagine you're sitting across a table for the first time from someone you don't know – a potential client, say. You've done all your due diligence (research) yet you're pretty likely to be surprised by who is sitting across from you. And the other way around. Bob Burg, author of Endless Referrals said in his book, "All things being equal, people will do business with, and refer business to, those people they know, like and trust." I wholeheartedly agree.

It is no coincidence that most of my customers are African-American women. I connect with their experiences without saying a word. Business is not only done in the board room.

My business like most businesses finds potential clients where we spend our leisure time – working with children in the education field, referrals by other clients, at the masjid or at various running events. The relationship with my clients mirrors all other relationships. There is a level of trust that has to be built and respectful communication.

McGraw-Hill published a great article on communication[29] and some of the inaccurate blunders that keep me gainfully working. First let's understand the model:

Sender The communication process begins with a **sender,** the person who transmits a message.

A **message** is any signal that triggers the response of a receiver. Some messages are deliberate, while others (such as sighs and yawns) are unintentional. Messages are not synonymous with meanings.

Encoding The sender must choose certain words or nonverbal methods to send an intentional message. This activity is called **encoding.** The words and channels that a communicator chooses to deliver a message can make a tremendous difference in how that message is received.

Channel The **channel** (sometimes called the **medium**) is the method used to deliver a message. As a business communicator, you have a world of choices, phone, mail, e-mail, facebook, a friend, etc..

Receiver A **receiver** is any person who notices and attaches some meaning to a message. In the confusing and imperfect world of business, however, several problems can occur. The message may never get to the receiver. Even worse, a message intended for one receiver might be intercepted by another one. A bystander might overhear your critical remarks about a co-worker, or a competitor might see a copy of your correspondence to a customer.

Decoding Even if a message does get to its intended receiver intact, there is no guarantee that it will be understood as the sender intended it to be. The receiver must still **decode** it, attaching meaning to the words or symbols. It is a mistake to assume that your messages will always be decoded accurately.

Feedback Receivers don't just absorb messages like sponges; they respond to them. Consider audience questions during a talk or the way a customer glances at the clock during a sales presentation. Imagine the tone of voice an employer might use while The discernible response of a receiver to a sender's message is called **feedback.** Some feedback is nonverbal—smiles, sighs, and so on. Sometimes it is oral, as when you react to a colleague's ideas with questions or comments. Feedback can also be written, as when you respond to a co-worker's memo. In many cases, *no* message can be a kind of feedback. Failure to answer a letter or to return a phone call can suggest how the non communicative person feels about the sender.

Around 2 months ago, I realized adding soft, communication skills is the next level in my business. Based on my own communication style this was a task I could not handle alone so I teamed up with some of the best communicators I know, so WE can do the work. Teaching businesses how to partner (which means a new plateau of trust exists) and communicate with the goal of generating more revenue in their businesses for a win-win situation is the work. Fortunately, I lived in Washington, D.C. and they knew how to do the work. Now is the time to work on me by communicating well within the team so we can be the model that is copied. We have to put in the work because ALL business with the required trust and respectful communication is very, very personal.

Quote #36 "Time is Money." - by Benjamin Franklin

One of the biggest problems I see with women business owners is that they don't value their time. Some business owners incorrectly assume that if their business is not paying them, their time is worthless. The value of a person's time is not related to how much the business can afford to pay them. Those are the type of people who measure their worth by their income. Usually when I asked how much does it cost your business to run on a monthly basis, 80% of the time, women business owners don't include themselves as a cost of business. So they count extremely low overheads. They tend not to put a price on their time, invariably they are always pricing themselves too low. When this "discounted price" is relayed to the prospective buyer, unlike myself who buys on value, the customer usually walks away. This is quite shocking to the business owner. The business owner expects more customers at low prices but they actually receive less customers. Why? From the customers prospective, low prices mean cheap. People know buying things cheaply will cost them more, with replacement costs and more time spent on shopping in the long run so they tend to walk away from the potential deal.

A few years ago, I was reflecting on the good times I had as a child with my mother. My mother had a daughter who turned into a wonderful friend. My mother also thought she had one daughter but wind up with collection of friends who made a community for each other and their children. I asked my mother, who spent quite a lot of time with me - "Do you have any regrets?" She said, "I regret that I did not spend more time with you." wow.

To me, my mother was and still is the smartest person I know. She moved us out of poverty Alhamdulillah, by not allowing the poverty mindset to set in. She would tell me then we are not poor, we are broke – there is a difference. The P.O.O.R. (passing over opportunity repeatedly) mindset comes from impoverished people who lack the desire for sustainable means of revenue outside of the wonderful government assistance programs. Those are folks who are P.O.O.R. Pass Over Opportunity Repeatedly but have all the time in the world to do nothing or what's worse is the use their precious words to destroy other people's (like their children's) dreams. On the other side of the coin are the workaholics, i.e. middle class folks, who slave at their jobs 5-7 days a week and have no time to spend the money they are earning.

Every few years, we moved like the Jeffersons to a bigger and better place. My mom worked long hours but made sure I did not want to get caught up in the rat race. She would say things like "you can have time or you could have money but you could not have both." She would also say "live beneath your means" and she told me "children are the greatest possession and nothing matters but the welfare of your children." She said this to me when I had no children at all.

Islam has definitely changed my view of the world with the very traditional roles of men and women. My mom said "You can be anything you want to be, you just have to work for it." I embraced what I learned from my mom and worked for the things I desired but motherhood halted "things" I desired. How did that happen?

It happened because of a few incidences in my short life. For one, my mom told me that over time in a 9 to 5 job, companies pay their employees less over time. In most white collar job, employees are not paid on an hourly basis but are paid on a salary that does not account for a maximum but a minimum number of hours. For example, when a person is just learning the job they might start at 40,000 and work 40 hours a week so the hourly rate is 40,000/2,000 hours = 20.00 per hour. As they get more experience in years 3 - 6, they get a raise but the number of hours also increases. In this example, now they make 48,000 per year but they work 60 hours a week so they actually make 48000/3000 = 16.00 per hour - a 20% DECREASE in salary!! That is why I never stayed at any job more than 4 years! The employee usually stays at the job because it is easier to stay at that job then use the time and energy to find a new job. In my new job, I worked less hours because I was new and only took jobs which paid a higher salary.

The second incident took me a while to understand. During my days at Temple University, I double majored in Management Information Systems, Risk Management and Insurance with a minor in Human Resources. We used to look at the actuary tables which insurers use to calculate with accuracy the number of people (insureds) who are predicted to die at a certain ages. Here I was at the age of 20 calculating the likelihood of my own death. I had all the risk factors besides smoking of an early death according to the actuary tables. I was African-American with a lower life expectancy, who was overweight with hypertension which is precursor to heart disease.

After being on hypertension medication for 13 years, I found out with the birth of my second child that I had literally been drugged by the medical system. Because I was taking an aspirin pill a day during my pregnancy, on my doctor's orders, my son was born G6PD deficient. If he has an aspirin or fava beans, he will die. Wow. Doctors are designed to medicate patients which profits the industry instead of finding out the cause of the problem. They put you on one drug then give you another drug to cover-up the side effects from the first drug. These drugs are not natural to our bodies. The side effects are signs to get off the drugs! Effectively, we are just buying into a corrupt system. In other words, the cause of the hypertension was the stress of my life. So instead of needing a doctor, I needed a therapist to help me balance by finding another way to live.

Knowing that I was predicted to die an early death and the wisdom from my mom is how I learned to value my time. According to my own values and the priorities of Islam, the time with my family is more valuable than the time I was spending at work. The time that I was spending away from my children was actually costing me WAY more than I was willing to pay. I had to find a way, like most single moms in Philadelphia, to combine my ability to generate revenue for my family AND spend quality time with my children. That is the best of both worlds that I was taught I could not have - I wanted time and money.

In business, you will get more money if your respect your own time. That is one of the reasons, women still earn 76 cents to every man's dollar – a statistic that has not changed in the last 10 years. So, I have no time to waste. It is my business to teach other women how to value their time and get the best of both the time and money worlds.

Marketers will tell every business owner, not to compete on price because that is ALWAYS a losing battle. There will always be someone cheaper so every business (i.e. person) must learn to differentiate themselves in a different way.

Quote #37 "Some men can run the fastest, jump the highest, or lift the heaviest, but no man has the corner on ambition, desire, and hustle." - by Author Unknown

This is part 2 of the mind of an entrepreneur - How to move from hustle mode to True Business. I am a consultant. As with any new project, we start with an assessment. An assessment helps to answer the question "Where is the business now?" As I have said many times, the issue with small businesses is that they think too small. The limits on the personal vision limit the vision of the business. The vision answers the question "How far does the owner want the business to grow?"

I am also a product of my environment. My vision expanded by what I saw when my mother started her clothing business in my youth. She did not try to do it as a side hustle. She took all the risk and quit her job, set up an 800 number in her home office, invested in a few sewing machines and hired a seamstress to make the clothes. She was not trying to be a one woman show. I am also greatly influenced by my mother and her expectations of me. I knew by the age of 4 that I was going to college. I did not say expected to go, for that was not her expectation. I was going and there was no decision, on my part, not to. My mother did not graduate from college because she chose to have me. I am a part of her dream deferred. Unlike the way other people raise their children, I was expected to be better than her at everything. She also expected that her achievements were the floor of my achievements and there was no ceiling.

Now is the time to break out of the shell and open up the can of worms. What is the motivation to quit the easy life of working 9 to 5 for a steady paycheck to give up valuable time by investing in a business. If the goal is financial, than honesty it is just plain easier to go back to work. Financial goals won't sustain the business when the times get rough, the hours are long and the money is short. Financial goals are very short-sighted. People with financial goals won't invest in the business for long term success. They won't incorporate their business, they won't open a business bank account, they won't get a professional e-mail address and they won't do anything that costs money. Those are exactly the people who start "side hustles."

My why is to build sustainable entities with employment opportunities for future generations that build economic empowerment for the minority population in the Philadelphia community, specifically, the West Philadelphia community. All this said was that I am trying to build a company to leave to my children so they are not dependent on Corporate America feeling sorry for them and handling them a piece of a pitiful job. In other words, I don't want my children being adults and working in fast food restaurants trying to survive.

As I was building my business, I realized this is just a system that can be shared and duplicated for any business. So, step 1 is to know your why and step 2 is to put systems in place. Business can be described as a three legged stool. The first leg is the marketing to find customers, the second leg is the product/service, and the third leg is the financing to build the product and pay the suppliers until the product is delivered to the customer. Each of the legs require a system.

Marketing is a systematic set of events designed to generate a positive return on your investment. As with everything, preparation is key. Make a plan and then hire other resources to help execute the plan.

A business starts with an accounting system. Quickbooks is too complicated for a small business and that is why I highly recommend the FREE accounting tool Freshbooks[7]. Freshbooks started out as an online invoicing system to help clients pay your business fast but it can also load expenses to generate a weekly, monthly or yearly Profit/Loss Report. If you can't track your business, then YOU HAVE NO BUSINESS! Once an accounting system is in place, generate a marketing budget which will help measure return on investment for every marketing decision! If you are starting a business with no money then you are not ready to start a business. They say "it takes money to make money" for a reason. Using my mothers' theory to live beneath my means, I had assets that were available to a single mom with three young children. I also took a calculated risk with my job by working part time to build the prospect list.

What I learned is that a business should have

- marketing strategy,

- budget,

- website,

- logo,

- professional business email address (not gmail, yahoo, aol, comcast, etc.),

- at least three testimonials,

- Mission statement/or unique value proposition before they officially open for business!

Tory Johnson writes on Fox Small Business[8], that

"Step 4 is What will it cost? Determine how much it will cost to start the business, and how much can be charged for the product or service, Have some formula of how much is needed to make in a year with X amount of clients or products sold. Without the numbers, there is no business.

Step 5 is don't get stuck in planning mode. This is easy to do, especially when starting out. The spark doesn't happen in planning mode, it happens when they are taking action to start building a business.

Step 6 is to determine success. Have some type of measurable benchmarks in place for the business to determine success. Holding the owner accountable for these measurements will enable them to tweak and work out the kinks in the model."

Business owners are wise to invest in their business which is an investment in themselves. These are a few of the key steps needed to move from the "side hustle" into true business.

Quote #38 "Plans are nothing; *planning is everything."* – by Dwight D. Eisenhower

They say "the most successful people are good at plan B." There are too many unknowns in life to get mad at everything at does not go according to "YOUR" plan. We don't own a thing in this world so what makes anyone think that the world should move with them or to even think someone or something is moving against them. I feel so safe in knowing that I am a microscopic molecule that has no bearing in the master plan. What I am guided to do quite simply is to survive the tests of this life using the religious rules of Islam in preparation for the next chapter. This does not mean that I don't plan. I spend a lot of time planning my day and organizing tasks to become an efficient multi-tasker. As the unknowns become known, I have to adjust my day and my plans accordingly. The life of a single mom of three children is full of curve balls that I am trying to negotiate. My plans, as all plans should be, are subject to change. That is why this quote is so good. The plans HARDLY EVER GO ACCORDING TO PLAN. More than 9 times out of ten, an unknown happens and most people are not reacting to the new plan but are stuck disappointed that the expected plan did not happen! American Express wrote that in business[9], "The plan becomes gospel—inviolable, non-negotiable and non-optional. This dynamic—managing fiercely against a plan that comes out of a process we have little faith in—results in dysfunctional management. It is foolish to engage in planning on the assumption that the plan you come up with will play out as you want. In fact, you can be confident that it won't.

Truth is, as Mike Tyson once said, "Everyone has a plan until you hit them in the jaw." Or, as Napoleon put it, "No plan survives contact with the enemy." The point of planning is not the plan itself—the point is to develop an understanding of what's likely to happen in the future, and to be fully prepared for most circumstances. No professional golfer plays a practice round with the idea in their head that they will play the competition rounds precisely the same. They play practice rounds to be fully prepared for any eventuality on match day: What happens if I go in that bunker, land on that part of the green, miss that fairway?

Here are three ways you can make planning a powerful, vibrant process in and of itself—and get better plans as a result.

1. Embrace the process. See the planning process itself (not the resulting plan) as the main thing. Invest time to do it right. Get the right people in the room. Ask a great facilitator to help you. Roll around in the process. Luxuriate in it. Get good at it.

2. Plan to scenarios, not data points. Most people produce plans with, for example, a single projected revenue line—or if pushed, a "bad, better, best" range of projections. Sadly, life doesn't play out in single data points—it plays out in scenarios. When you're planning, start by putting together four or five likely scenarios as well as a few unlikely scenarios for your business next year: What happens if your key input cost rises 5 percent in a down market? Or your main customer goes elsewhere? Or you outgrow your existing store capacity? Plan against these, and rehearse your likely responses, so when one of them does happen, you know precisely how you're going to respond.

3. Bring the accountants in at the end. Most people start with the numbers and work backward: "I want to see a budget that shows 10 percent growth this year." Nothing happens like that in the real world. The tills don't fill up before the customers arrive—quite the opposite. Make your scenario-based plans first, then have the accountants work up the numbers. When you see the results, you might need to go back and re-plan your responses to some of the scenarios, but that's a good thing."

This means not to plan to a financial position (i.e. data point) but make plans to what if scenarios. The plan is to be brought out IF the scenario happens. Let's make this concrete with an example. There is no point in planning to lose XX pounds (i.e. data point) if there is no change in diet and lifestyle. It would be better to make a plan to exercise 3 times a week and stay away from carbohydrates after 7 pm at night than to make a plan to lose 10, 30 or 80 pounds. When a person can see the difference in that plan, then they are on the right track for a better planning process and that is the point of the quote.

Quote #39 "Wealth is a state of mind." - by Author Unknown

The business dictionary defines wealth as tangible or intangible thing that makes a person, family, or group better off. In the capitalistic society of the United States, most people seek to obtain financial (tangible) wealth as a goal. After the death of my first born son, my mom gave me Sarah ban Breathnach's book titled "Simple Abundance" to help me work through the state of depression. It took some time for me to understand that I was living in abundance but at that time, I did not appreciate the abundance of love (intangible) that I had from my parents, my friends and my mother's family. As I described in my first book, my mother and her family experienced losses of life multiple times throughout the years. My mother's father, my grandfather, passed away when my mother was only 4 years old. In 1971 on what they call "thanksgiving day" her family experienced an electrical fire that destroyed the house and killed 7 of my cousins ages 4 months to the age of 12 and my grandmother's' best friend forever. Our family was used to pain and out of the pain came a love of life that I thought was normal. Didn't every family come into homes free of tension, free of arguments, free of envy? It is an abundance of love that makes me wealthy MashaAllah.

I am an expert at social media. Says who? I do. I am beautiful. Says who? I do. I am wealthy Says who? I do. That is why my mother said "You can be anything YOU want to be." Claire Amber and I agree that "wealth is a state of mind" therefore I choose to be wealthy (see my mommy was right). Claire Amber writes in elephantjournal.com[10] that, "Are you dealing with a poverty mentality? If so, what can you do to cultivate a feeling of overall abundance? Well, I'll give you three tips.

1. Let go of anything that doesn't feel abundant to you, that does not make your heart rejoice, that you never use, etc. Do this as a means of calling life force energy back into your life, and hold that as your intention, as you do so. When you're done, you'll be surrounded by things that you love and you will have made a vacuum for good things to come in!

2. Learn to enjoy the journey, live in the moment and appreciate all that you have… even the most basic things, that support you in your life every day.

3. Focus on your spiritual connection and begin to make your choices from a place of love, rather than fear. Tune into your heart more often. Be generous with your time and love, and look at the world in terms of what you have to offer."

Having abundance is wealth. When we have cultivated these principles in life, there is an equal opportunity of the wealthy mindset that enriches not only our lives but also the lives of those around us. My children and your children are worth fighting for to live in "simple abundance" that has been redefined as wealth.

Quote #40 "Leadership is Influence." - by John C. Maxwell

Thought leaders have tried to define leadership for many years. Kevin Kruse of Forbes wrote in his article[31], "Leadership has nothing to do with seniority or one's position of hierarchy of a company" and I agree. "Leadership has nothing to do with titles," my mom told me that years ago. "Leadership has nothing to do with personal attributes" says the word leaders and what most people think of take-charge domineering individuals. I don't agree with that. Leadership most certainly deals with the "make-up of a man" we call character. Bill Gates said "Leaders will be those who empower others." I agree with that statement but that is just part of leadership. Kevin Kruse says "Leadership is the process of social influence, which maximizes the efforts of others, towards achievement of a goal." For me, my mentor and John C. Maxwell, "Leadership is influence." The ability to influence comes from certain positions/titles in society. If the position automatically becomes the decision maker, the person with the title is influential in the decision.

For example, I am the head of my household. The title of mom says I can positively or negatively affect those three children around me. Because I chose incorrectly to become a single mom, this position carries great personal (not communal) responsibility. As many of my readers know, because I want things my way all the time (and I am still working on that), this was the path I chose so I could bear all the responsibility without having to share my decisions or my thought processes. What I found out is that it is too much responsibility for one person to bear. When it is done properly, it is a shared responsibility between two people with a communal (family) support system. So, the title delegates much responsibility. My children and my capacity to be responsive to their needs have actually been quite influential on me. After the birth of my third child, I realized quickly that it was too much to bear and willingly shared my weaknesses to find and secure a support system. For some reason, my support system had been there for many years, I just hadn't noticed it. Once my eyes opened to the team who had been there all along, I experienced a "change of heart" and worked hard to be the giver that most people see now. It was a transition as I had to learn how to navigate my responsibilities to positively influence those around me. In essence, my children have made me become a better leader in the home and outside of the home.

The journey to Islam was one of influence. I was led to the righteous path by my BFF and her family. The influence started when I was just 8 years old but I did not formally embrace Islam until I was 37! We shared a whole lifetime of the ups and downs of friendship. Her influence had nothing to do with reciting surahs (chapters) of the Quran, it had nothing to do with telling me the religious rules. It had everything to do with her personal integrity and character and the beauty of the light she carried within. We knew even as children and teenagers that if she was with us, the meat had to be halal. There was no other way. Even though we were not Muslim at the time, it was the respect of our friendship and her religion that caused us to change. I have always wanted my way all the time but I would listen to her because she was living like I wanted to live. She had her own business, she owned her home, she was making moves. When I first had the idea to start my business, I had a friend who I could take advice from and she was the first person I called. That is why I agree that "leadership is influence" and why I would say leadership has everything to do with character.

People without good character can't become leaders. The untrustworthy can never be leaders because they have given up on their "word." The receiving person in the leadership conversation won't trust what the untrustworthy person has to say. It is good character that makes one become a leader not the other way around. Some people mistakenly believe that becoming a leader will make them have good character. That is like saying having a bachelor's degree will make someone become smart. The person had to be smart to earn a bachelor's degree. The work of becoming a person with good character, like all other things in life, comes first. As you can see, my journey was not to become a leader, it was to be influenced by others to make me a better mother and a better person. Leadership was a byproduct of doing the work. I find much reward in doing the work :-)

Quote #41 "Business is a Marathon, not a Sprint" - by Author Unknown

"Business is not a question of will I fail but WHEN will I fail. What happens next is your choice." #thechoiceisyours - by Ed Gordon

Todd Knutson said

"I wrote about the importance of getting away from ad agency new business to get refreshed and re-energized. But there's more to it: it is taking a long-term view of the work you do. As a former long distance runner, I often describe work as a marathon, not a sprint. This metaphor helps me to pace myself, set goals, train properly, set realistic deadlines, and think.

Here's what I mean:

- Pace: Unless you're an elite runner, you can't sprint a marathon. If you do, you'll burn out. The same applies to work. If you work seven days a week as hard as you can, before too long your productivity will plummet.
- Goals: Runners set many goals: total miles per week, time per mile, miles for long runs, short runs, etc. Goals for new business might include calls per day, conversations per day, hours spent researching; number of networking meetings, first meetings, RFPs submissions per month; wins per quarter; win rates, etc.
- Training: Marathon runners often train 5-6 days a

week. They run in the rain, snow, heat and wind. Nothing stops them. Do you train that rigorously at work? Most of us do initially, but then settle into our routines. Are you creating new challenges weekly? Monthly? Are you training for your next job, and training someone to replace you?

- Realistic Deadlines: Runners plan to run a marathon in the future, because they know it takes time to prepare. At work, think about setting deadlines for yourself and your team that are challenging, yet realistic. Occasional sprints can be great for team building, building your culture, and overall morale. However, too many "invented crises" will wear you out.

- Time to Think: Beside the endorphin rush, for me the best part of running was letting my mind go. I would often head out for a run when faced with a difficult problem. By the time I got back, I'd figured it out. You can't do this when you're sprinting. Similarly, at work, you if you're always head-down sprinting - fighting fires, or dealing with client or employee issues - you won't have time to think. Perhaps you can block quiet time off on your calendar, or go for a walk at lunch or schedule workouts a few times each week.

Success comes in many forms, but one thing is certain: if you burn out early any success will be short-lived. You may find that thinking about work as a marathon will build your endurance and productivity.

Quote #42 "I don't care how much power, brilliance or energy you have, if you don't harness it and focus it on a specific target, and hold it there you're never going to accomplish as much as your ability warrants." - by Zig Ziglar

"The successful warrior is the average man with Laser-like focus." - by Bruce Lee

In my "bra burning" past, I had no clue about gender roles. Women and men are supposed to be treated differently because they are different! Women can't talk about pay equality when women won't admit the undocumented benefits received (like doors are supposed to be open for us, men should want to provide for us, etc...) just for being women. My mother said "American women are the luckiest women in the world." We enjoy freedoms that most women in the world can not even fathom. What I have learned in my quest for "freedom" is that I have sacrificed too much. I sacrificed marriage which included stability and a male figure as head of household for a career and motherhood. Danielle Crittenden wrote in the book, "What our Mothers Didn't tell Us," on page 74 that "A woman will not understand what true dependency is until she is cradling her own infant in her arms; nor will she likely achieve the self-confidence she craves until she has withstood, and transcended, the weight of responsibility a family places upon her -- a weight that makes all the paperwork and assignments of her in-basket seem feather-light." Stephen R. Covey said "Many people seem to think that success in one area can compensate for failure in other areas. But can it really?...True effectiveness requires balance." So, the journey to find balance continues while using the power of focus.

Canfield and co-authors Mark Hansen and Les Hewitt recommend that we concentrate on our strengths, set goals, and focus on them. Canfield and Hansen wrote the Chicken Soup for the Soul series, which now has 27 titles and has sold 47.5 million copies. Canifield wrote in The Power Focus book's notes that[32], "The No. 1 reason that stops people from getting what they want is lack of focus. People who focus on what they want, prosper. Those who don't, struggle. In The Power of Focus you'll discover the specific focusing strategies used by the world's most successful men and women. Find out how to: -Focus on your strengths and eliminate everything that is holding you back. -Change bad habits into habits that will make you debt-free and wealthy. -Build an excellent balance between work and family life - without guilt! Your ability to focus will determine your future - start now!" The book writes plain and simple, the only purpose of the book is to inspire you to take action.

Proper focus allows a person to weed out distractions. Discipline is a result of daily habits. It is the daily habits that become actions. Those action steps are the key to success in this life. They say "small actions add up to large results." I actually look forward to the thirty day fast during the month of Ramadan. That is where I practice the power of changing my habits. Now that I have lived three years as a Muslimah (female Muslim), I make it a habit to fast throughout the year so that the 30 days during Ramadan are easier. Then fasting becomes part of a habit. Stephen Covey wrote in The 7 Habits of Highly Effective People: Powerful Lessons in Personal Change that, "Habit is the intersection of knowledge (what to do), skill (how to do), and desire (want to do)." In the Power of Focus, they say "Habits come from repeating a behavior until is becomes easy." For people who are called into the religion of Islam, praying five times a day daily makes it a habit that becomes easy. Over time that leads to a changed person. For example, changing habits 4 times per year leads to 20 changes over 5 years - see that's very easy and as my teacher would say "good for you." Sean Covey wrote in "The 7 Habits Of Highly Effective Teens" that "We become what we repeatedly do." The power of FOCUS is knowing what a person wants to do. Bruce Lee is credited with saying "The successful warrior is the average man with laser-like focus."

Some people get so caught up in their habits, they don't take the time to think through what they do repeatedly. This is where we use self-evaluation or in my case reflection comes into play. We have to write down our habits and what would we like to change. The change is what habits would we like to improve upon. That is the game-plan. The book, "The Power of Focus" says "make a habit of changing your habits."

It is easier to use evaluation when a person allows other people to be a mirror and reflect on a person's behavior. Stephen R. Covey is quoted as saying, "Interdependence is a choice only independent people can make." I allowed my mentor to evaluate me. I must note that he was a mentor to hundreds of other people at the same time! So, when I knew he would be at a location, I showed up. He chose to take me on as a mentee because he saw potential in me that I could not "see." This is where most people, in general, fail and accept the status quo. Stephen Covey is also quoted as saying, "Treat a man as he is and he will remain as he is. Treat a man as he can and should be and he will become as he can and should be." My mentor expected me to become better and raised the bar on acceptable habits. That is my intention in working with others and also what I expect in people who work with me. The journey continues on changing habits to focus on becoming a better version of me.

Quote #43 "Communication is Key." - by Nicole Newman

I started Newman Networks with the idea that information was being delivered on the super highway called the internet and entire minority groups were being left behind. I thought there was a technology gap but it turns out to be a communication gap. We all know and expect that learning happens between a student and a teacher. It is has been researched and shown that students learn from teachers who look like them. Women learn more from women and men learn more from men. I know now that as a single mother, I can not raise a boy to be a man which is why I am thankful for the Jawala Scouts, a manhood development organization. This is also why men are being actively recruited to teach boys. This is not true of just children but it is also true of adults. So, the issue that my company was trying to solve is help more people use the information superhighway to build cost-effective businesses through networking.

My thinking was that we needed women who could get other women business owners to understand new technologies. Having a teacher that looks like the student, allows the student to build trust quickly through unspoken communication. Therefore, the Philadelphia economy would not suffer from minority groups, which are the majority, being left behind. This is when I found out that we did not have a technology issue but we have a communication issue. Not understanding technology is a symptom of the communication problem. If we now focus on fixing communication issue we can work on a myriad of problems that affect our community like expectations on the job which is a part of growing a business or expectations inside our homes which is a part of growing strong families. What hurts our communication style is that we don't trust what the other party is saying because we are used to being taken advantage of. So, every communication becomes suspect to what we assume is a person's true intentions.

It is unfortunate that most people have been taken advantage of. The mistrust did not stop at the situation but it is brought into every new relationship. That is the baggage that we carry around in our spoken and unspoken communications. They say "most communication is not verbal."

Lee Froschheiser wrote on the Reliable Plant Website[33] that, "Regardless of whether you're talking about business, politics, sports or the military, the best leaders are first-rate communicators. Their values are clear and solid, and what they say promotes those values. Their teams admire them and follow their lead. Likewise, if you want your company to reach new benchmarks of achievement, you must master the art of clear communication. So, how do you do it? First, you must realize and accept that clear communication is always a two-way process. It is not enough to speak clearly; you have to make sure you're being heard and understood. To facilitate this, use the following two-way communication primer:

Prepare how you'll communicate

• Clarify the goal of the communication.

• Plan carefully before sending it or meeting in person.

• Anticipate the receiver's viewpoint and feelings.

Deliver the message

• Express your meaning with conviction.

• Relate the message to your larger goals.

• Identify the action to be taken.

• Confirm the other person understands.

Receive the message

• Keep an open mind.

• Identify key points in the message.

• Value constructive feedback and use it to grow.

• Confirm your understanding.

Evaluate the effectiveness of the communication afterwards

Take corrective action as necessary."

The objective of Newman Networks is to focus on technology as a communication tool for economic empowerment for the majority community in Philadelphia. I am blessed because as they say "iron sharpens iron." I work with some of the best women communicators who are dedicated to the cause Alhamdulillah!

Quote #44 "Word is bond." - by Author Unknown

There are some well established guidelines in business. This one is pretty old "Word is bond." Quite simply do what you say you are going to do. Since you said it, keep your word and do it. Whether it means keeping an appointment, whether it means paying a supplier by a certain date or whether it means establishing bed time for your children. Your word sets the expectations in the other parties mind. The other party does not have to be a customer and they can be young or old. This is the bond of communication and how trust is built or trust is broken. If a person can't keep their word, they are deemed by the other party as untrustworthy which breaks the bond built by communicating the expectation. Like Bob Burg famously said in his quote, from the book Endless Referrals, "All things being equal, people will do business with, and refer business to, those people they know, like and trust."

This is especially true with small businesses. Most of their business comes from word of mouth (i.e. referrals) and great small businesses understand that their reputation precedes them and work hard to build, maintain and grow their reputation by keeping their word. Keeping a person's word builds trust and loyalty. Keeping a person's word builds confidence that no means no and yes means yes. It becomes cut and dry. They say "When you operate with integrity, hard decisions become easy." I once was told by a highly respected mentor that I had too much integrity for business! From their perspective in the capitalistic society of the United States, business was built on cheating one another. For example, the American culture celebrates the taking of the land from the native American Indians and calls it "Thanksgiving" which millions of immigrants celebrate while denying other immigrants access to the stolen land. How crazy is that? To tell others to operate with integrity while one does not "eat their own medicine" is hypocrisy and it is to be avoided. Hypocrisy breaks the bond of communication provided in the word.

Since I have embraced Islam, my religion matches my integrity and allows me to raise the bar and not work for money but the ultimate goal of Jennah (paradise/heaven) Alhamdulillah! Not working for money does not mean that I do not get paid for services rendered. The payment for service is respect of the value proposition provided by time, inspiration, knowledge and the network.

Word is bond also does not mean that the word (i.e. communication) can not be changed. It just has to be communicated in a way that sets a new or different expectation. For example, if a person expects an arrival at 10:00 am and the conditions change so that the other party will not arrive until 10:15 am, then the other party is EXPECTED to call. That keeps the bond of trust that has to be in place for the lines of communication (i.e. marketing) to stay open and grow. This reminds me that I need to cancel my 2:30 appointment today:-). In the technology age that we live in, this process has become much easier to do. The system that I use is the Google calendar that can be accessed from any device (tablet, computer, phone) to keep my schedule and my three children's schedule aligned. My clients and potential clients are not allowed to get on the schedule usually between 3pm and 6pm, Friday afternoons or Sunday mornings. Those are reserved for family time. My business which is what we call my life, works better when there is a balance and order between religion, family and work.

Word is bond becomes especially important as the business grows. We said "no man (or business) is an island." This bond has to be tight with the team members in the business so that the business can grow. Those people that are "hard to work with" can not grow a business. Those people that are "untrustworthy" can not communicate to build relationships with others. Business and life requires that we work with people who are not inanimate objects to be played with! Word is bond can only be achieved when people respect the values brought on or added by other people. Without the respect of the other parties EXPECTATIONS; words are easily broken, there is a lack of commitment and Philadelphians have lost economic empowerment opportunities for their youth. The cycle of hopelessness continues which is why it is up to US to save US by committing to our word which earns respect and builds TRUST. It is that simple.

Quote #45 "Though no one can go back and make a brand new start anyone can start from now and make a brand new ending." - by Carl Bard.

"It Doesn't Matter Where You Start, Just Start." - by Author Unknown

They say "Start where you are, use what you have, do what you can." As with everything it starts with an intention. Intention is what you allow in the mind to determine the actions. People usually change course when the pain is unbearable or they want to achieve a different result.

You have to believe that the goal is not impossible for you but possible because of YOU. Most of the time, people don't believe in themselves because of what other people have told them during their youth that has been internalized way into adulthood. We have to believe in ourselves and that happens by passing the tests of life. My mentor would say "The greatest hurdle one faces is the 6 inches between a person's ears." I believe that we are all made to enrich each others lives through our unique blessings AND shortcomings. When we can recognize our own shortcomings, we open ourselves to receiving the blessings sent by Allah for improvement. And yes, I don't believe in self-improvement or self-made millionaires. We are born into a family unit so how can anything be self-made?

"They say it doesn't matter where you start, just start." No matter how young or old, able or disabled, short or tall, thin or fat, humble or conceited, grateful or ungrateful, we are able to start again. Someone once judged me and said "You are like this and there is nothing you can do about it because you are made already." I knew right then that that's how that person thinks about themselves - locked in someone's box because I can and have transformed my thoughts to those things which benefit me and my family. I still have a long way to go but I can reflect while on the journey to see not only where I am going but also where I have been Alhamdulillah!

A facebook friend said to me just today that "I write well." My response was "MashaAllah You made my day! My mother is the writer in my family. This does not come natural for me but like anything I commit to, I make the intentions and practice. To think I only received a 440 on the English SAT and had to take remedial English in college to now writing books." We have been blessed with a new day, are you ready to start?

Quote #46 "People quit their boss, not their job." - by Author Unknown

My mother worked in corporate America during my entire childhood. She had many bosses but the bosses who gave her the most trouble were women specifically, African-American women. My mother used to tell me that "there can only be ONE queen bee" and I promised when I was young that I would never to be an overbearing, micromanaging supervisor. I was blessed because as an Information Technology employee we earned a lot of leeway on the job. Our jobs required us to think and so the "cigarette breaks" were extra long. On one of my jobs, I was expected to take an hour and a half for lunch so I wouldn't look any different from the other workers who took an hour and half for lunch. Eventually, I did become a boss and through trial and error I learned to value employees. They don't have to work for me. It is a choice and just like I choose not to work for money, they also can choose not to work with me. It has happened before so it will likely happen again.

Businesspaths.net says[34], "A popular belief is that the primary reason people quit their jobs is because of pay. Not so according to a Gallup poll of more than one million employed U.S. Workers. A bad boss or supervisor is the number one reason people leave due to the environment their boss makes and how they feel they've been treated." The article then goes on to say "So, it is important to find an environment where we feel valued and have meaningful work to do. Employees want the opportunity to learn and grow and work for a manager who encourages and supports excellence in all they do. The truth is...people want to make a difference. And, in return they want to be treated with dignity and respect, have some influence over their future and feel appreciated for their contributions. People thrive when they are part of a winning organization. They have pride in the products and services being offered, they know they can satisfy customer needs and are confident they can positively impact the success of the organization."

That is what I found worked at Deloitte Touche Tomatsu. I was apart of a winning organization and it was hard but rewarding work. I did not make the most money at the job but it gave me a sense of satisfaction. I had "made it" and had a view at the top but I did not like what I was sacrificing to get there. Business is made of talented teams - there are no employers and employees. There are teams of people working together to reach a common goal. The team lead must set an environment that is conducive to success by aligning the environment with: employee involvement (responsibility), meaningful work (a sense of purpose) and professional development (evaluation, critiques and encouragement).

The article says and I concur that the organization must:

1) Value The Employees - Your employees need to know that leadership places as much value in them as they do in their customers.

2) Lead and Engage Your People - Leadership is vital to engaging people and delivering results. Leaders need to communicate clear direction and priorities, let people know what's expected, and regularly share how they are doing against expectations. This helps people see how what they do contributes to the success of the team and organization.

3) Provide Meaningful Work - People enjoy spending their time performing tasks and working on projects that have a significant impact.

4) Ensure Learning and Development - Organizations must provide opportunities for their employees to learn and grow. They regularly coach and provide feedback to their people on how they are doing so they know where to focus their improvement efforts. They also take the time to catch people in the act of doing things right, and provide recognition for a job well done.

The article ends by stating "If you want to attract the right people and retain star performers, it is important to recognize that your people are your most valuable asset!" I am set to prove my mother wrong through building a team with many African-American queen bees. It is seems very easy to do because I want for my sisters what I want for myself :-)

Quote #47 "No man is an Island." - by Michael Gerber, author of the e-Myth Revisited

Business is overwhelming. The quicker a business owner realizes they can't do it all by themselves the better! To work together, a level of trust must be built. Usually that trust factor is inherited from the family structure. That is how other cultures migrate from other countries and get off the boat to work together to start, build and sustain their businesses through their already inherited and maintained family structure.

If we want a sustainable economic base for African-Americans by redeveloping businesses in the Philadelphia community, we have to build and sustain better family structures. It is just that simple. This means I have to give up the independence my mother and grandmother fought for during the Women's Liberation Movement and to go back to my role of a helpmate to my husband. Readers have to understand that is a huge undertaking for me! Submitting to the will of Allah seems like an easy task compared to submitting to the will of my husband! Knowing what we have to do is half the battle, now I go and put in work. For there is much work to do!

Quote #48 We are kept from our goal not by obstacles but by a clear path to a lesser goal." - by Robert Brault

That is why we can not settle for good and must aspire for great. Complacency, which is accepting the lesser goal, kills dreams. Christopher Peterson writes in Psychology Today's article[35], "Goal Setting: Don't Pick the Low-Hanging Fruit." that "In the case of fruit, if it is hanging low, it may be bruised or damaged by bugs or varmints. It is also less likely to be ripe. Experienced fruit pickers always start at the top of a tree, where the fruit is more ready to eat because of greater exposure to the sun. And because a picker places fruit in a bag slung over his or her shoulder, the bag gets heavier as the job progresses, and starting at the top puts gravity on the side of the picker.

This essay is not really about fruit but about how we approach any and all tasks in our lives. Sometimes expediency gets in the way of efficiency and often in the way of excellence. If I want to cook a good meal, or prepare a good lecture, or be a good friend, whatever is low-hanging (in my refrigerator, in my mind, or in my heart) is not where I should start. Sometimes I take the easy way out, though, and I often regret it." They say "if you chose the easy door you made the wrong choice."

Quite simply, there is too much complacency going on in our hearts, our studies and our approach to life. The low hanging fruit that I was prepared for and accepted for a too long of time was the good paying job. I was not balanced. My job took me away from my family. I was willing to risk securities in material possessions like my money, my home, my 401K in a pursuit of happiness. I was searching for happiness not only for me but for my three young children. When I was unhappy, my children were unhappy. So, now that I have transitioned in my mind to that of a happy state with balance in my life, the next goal is to move others out of the state of complacency. We have been living in a matrix and every day we are given the choice, the red pill to free your mind or the blue pill to accept the status of this life.

As I reflect on the journey, I see it is working. My mother expected and would accept nothing less from me than to achieve more than she had. Instead of being the ceiling like I have seen in some families, her achievements were the floor. I was expected to go to college because she did not finish college when she became a parent. I was expected to make more money than she ever had because she wanted to prepare me for the financial responsibility of motherhood. It is funny because in the back of my mind I think about the book that she never published and now I am writing book #4. Complacency was not an option which is good because I am Ambitious with a capital A MashaAllah. When I moved on my block 9 years ago even though it is around the corner from a Masjid there were no Muslim families on the block. Now we have 3 families residing on the block to hopefully be examples by teaching values of respect for yourself and respect for others In sha Allah. We have to learn not to accept the low hanging fruit that is offered to people of color. It is up to us to save us by expecting and ONLY accepting what is good for ourselves and those around us. That is the example I saw in the practicing Muslim families that made Islam so attractive to me.

Quote #49 "You go, we go." - by Kurt Russell in Backdraft

As a computer programmer, I have worked in team environments almost my entire professional career. Some of the teams have been pretty bad where the people on the team constantly bickered between each other and some were outstanding where the goals of the team were more valued by all members of the team than individual goals. Even then there were conditions I did not tolerate. No talking about team members was a classic condition which was broken very often. One of the trade secrets I have used in the past was to make sure I tell people up front, I hold no secrets. If you don't want anyone to know, don't tell me. That way, people learned not to talk about other people around me. I did not like it then and I truly understand why it is sinful now. People who waste their time talking about other people can't be focused on the goals of making EVERYONE (including themselves and especially yours truly) better.

One of my good friends sent me a message a few weeks ago and asked if I was coming to class? I said no at the time but that message made me think. I made intentions to go to class and was so happy I did. I then sent her a message that said thanks for the push and she responded, if we are not pushing each other towards Jennah then we are not really friends. I soo love my sisters :-) This quote is one of my favorite lines in one of my favorite movies. "You go, we go" is said when Kurt

172

Russell could not hold on to his partner and instead of letting him go into the fire, they both fell because that is how committed they were to the goals of the team instead of the individualistic goal of looking out for self. "Crabs in the barrel" mentality is one of the downfalls of the African-American community, which is cultivated by parents talking about each other and that becomes the behavior that is modeled and accepted by our children.

One of my many parents used to talk about me in front of me, that way it was not backbiting. I finally had to tell this person, when you talk about me, you are really talking about yourself because I am a reflection of you. I have compassion for this parent because I know it is a learned behavior from their parent some 50+ years ago but I remind this person as I remind myself that we have to become conscious about what we teach and show our children. Somehow in the African-American community that I am apart of, we have lost the idea that our first team is our family. Embracing Islam helped me become more conscious of the family bond. I have learned over the last 3 years to cherish what my mother provided for me and turned my disappointment about expectations of my dad into appreciation. Looking at him from the sunny side up perspective has given us a better relationship. It also helps that I feel justified to lean on him even harder because I am single and therefore his responsibility until I find a husband.

In my innocence, I tried to build a trusted network where people did business with each other without a middleman or negotiator. That was the premise behind diversephilly.com. Usually the middle man is an extra cost. In computer terms, we called this role the liaison. I considered the middleman to be a bottleneck in the system. It just would be easier to do business without the need for a third party. I was just plain wrong. During the late 80's and early 90's this job was torn from the industry and now I can see how important that role has become. I know that most people are not good communicators because of their experiences and perceptions. People usually come into a business transaction with a code of unspoken language and unwritten rules. It is extremely difficult for conversations, let alone business to be transacted without a third party. Let's us not even say the P word as partnerships are nearly impossible. Now that I have the wisdom that a third party exists to make the communications between the parties run smoothly, I have had to brush up my own communication skills. Any work that makes me learn and disseminate what I learned is my favorite type of work!

Now, I have learned to communicate the goals of the team and work as the third party to uncover the unspoken language and unwritten rules that are the bottlenecks to the success of the team. As we all should know, business is built on teams and uncovering those unwritten rules and unspoken languages are also bottlenecks to the success of the family which is ultimately bottlenecks to the success of the community. What I need to understand and embrace is that the success of raising teams of families is a major factor in contributing to the economic success of my community. God willing more families will embrace the concept of "You go, we go."

Quote #50 "Happiness is when what you think and what you do and what you say are congruent." - by Mahamta Ghandi

They say "hurt me with the truth and never comfort me with a lie." Lies take away from my happiness. Mahamta Ghandi said "Happiness is when what you think and what you do and what you say are congruent." So, lies contribute to non-congruence and take away from happiness. For me and many other people, I was on a mission to find happiness. I wanted happiness in my life, happiness in my family, happiness in my work and happiness in my religion.

I find that most marriages are built upon lies and unrealistic expectations. There are those who believe that all men cheat. We have many discussions in the Early Bird Gets The Worm Facebook Group about this topic and I don't agree that all men cheat. I think that most men cheat because they need to feel good about themselves. Having another person outside of the lawful marriage makes them feel wanted and this is covering up the real issue of self-esteem. I am no different in that we all have issues. I use the crutch of food to deal with stress. But the men who choose not to cheat are not better men just because they are faithful. They could be weak in a different area. I think the man for me is the honest man. He can be honest about what he wants and truthful enough to share it with his cover in his wife.

For the honesty to happen, my goal in a relationship, which is TRUST, must be met. A Facebook friend said "I want to live in truth. Sometimes the truth hurts, but it is necessary. It's where trust starts." I replied "I completely agree.. without truth there is no trust. I value trust more than the pain of truth. Trust makes truth all worth it." So now we answer the question, How does one build trust?

Wikihow.com outlined 5 ways to build trust[36]:

Method 1 - Be Reliable

Method 2 - Be Honest

Method 3 - Be Open

Method 4 - Keeping confidences

Method 5 - Show Your Integrity

Be Reliable

Do what you say. Possibly the most important step in building a foundation of trust is to do what you say you will do. Even if it is a small thing, canceling or failing to follow through will build hairline fractures in your trustworthiness. Enough of those, and the foundation will crumble. This does not mean a person can't change but they have to clearly communicate, which means it must be stated by one party AND understood by the receiving party.

Honor all of your promises. Trust requires that people believe you are dependable. If you truly cannot meet the promise you've made, be decent enough to explain face-to-face why you can no longer do this. And don't just leave it there—make a new promise to make it up to that person.

Do not belittle the promise. However small and insignificant a promise may seem, realize that the other person may place much greater significance on the promise than you. Any lack of follow through will be hugely disappointing. Acknowledge their reality too before you break your promise.

Be Honest

Tell the truth. Sounds easy, right? Not always. It is surprisingly simple to find yourself saying a little white lie to protect your friend, lover, or even your parents. But if you tell the truth even when the truth isn't perfectly pleasant, you will become much more trustworthy.

Speak from the heart. Here is a tip when you really feel like lying to someone, either to spare their feelings or to spare yourself from their unfavorable response: Find an anchor point to focus on by choosing something good about that person. Speak to that goodness, rather than overplaying the bad news or reality check you need to convey. Focus on what the person does right and why this person matters. By doing this, you can cushion a blow and make it clear that you do not judge this person or the situation as indicative of any set outcome. Also, be sure to offer your willingness to listen.

Speak your feelings. People who only convey hard facts come across as cold and distant. While you may think it is easier to just regurgitate the facts as they happened (according to you), without a layer of compassion and understanding added to what you're conveying, people may perceive you as relishing another's distress. We are both emotional and rational beings and life is about balancing both, not being overly one way or the other.

Be Open

Volunteer information. When an opportunity to be vague arises, don't take it. Instead, volunteer information to your listener to prove that you have nothing to hide.

Don't omit important details. The main reason it is best not to omit important details is because it is hard to keep up with a string of omissions. People will start to notice contradictions in your stories and you will be considered a liar, even if you are only omitting a little! Tell people things they need or want to know. If you always provide reliable information, they will trust you.

If you do have secrets, let it be known. You shouldn't be forced to give up your most personal feelings and secrets just to be trustworthy. Everyone is entitled to privacy. But the key to being trustworthy while also maintaining your privacy is to make the boundary between what you're willing to share and what you want to keep to yourself clear.

Don't mask truths. An offshoot of "tell the truth" is never to mask truths. Sometimes it seems harmless to "morph" the truth into something more palatable to preserve your ego.

However well-meaning your intention, this is no better than a lie and will hurt trust.

Demonstrate that you expect reciprocal openness. Rely on the other person to give you the full truth. Mistrust comes as much from what people know, including what they do not know. Do not be afraid to ask question. Just take care not to come across as pushy or intimidating; always give your listener time to go off and think about their lack of openness toward you.

Keeping Confidences

Keep secrets imparted to you. No gossip allowed. Never blab someone else's story. Enough said. You can only trust people who are discreet and those who can keep the same silences or protect your confidences. If you tell, it will come back full circle and your confidante will cease to trust you.

If you do lie, admit to it. Sometimes it feels unavoidable to lie. It is best to confess to your lie as soon as possible and explain your motives. If you get caught, don't deny it. That is simply another lie.

Show Your Integrity

Display loyalty. This refers to your ability to protect others, to be on same side, both in their presence and, most importantly, in their absence. Trust is solid when a person knows he or she has your loyalty.

Be competent. Gain the respect and admiration of others by displaying adequate interpersonal skills and/or professional ability. Social skills and good manners can all be learned, even if you have social anxiety or other relating challenges. Do your best to practice basic social skills with people you trust, so that you can then help others who don't know you so well to trust you more.

Demonstrate a strong moral ethic. This is particularly important in relationships. The other person must feel confident that you will not falter or show betrayal in any form, even when away from each other. Be true and be dedicated.

Be neutral when placed in difficult predicaments. Do not choose sides until you make certain that you know the hard facts.

Do not display double standards. Show consistency in your behavior. Consistency in your behavior relates to your reliability and predictability. It also determines your ability and good judgment in handling situations. Be personally accountable for things that you're responsible for—do not try to shift the blame. If you are in a position of leading others, realize that the leader accepts blame on behalf of the team and does not attempt to shift it onto other people; this requires strength of character, so don't be afraid to start building yours up.

I never use the "keeping confidences" method. I am a marketer by profession so my job is to disseminate information. But I am "open" with vulnerabilities so I can tell people up front, don't tell me anything that cannot be shared. With leadership comes responsibility and it is our shared responsibility to be consistent with trust. Trust leads to happiness because that is when "what we think and what we do and what you say are congruent."

Quote #51 "If you want to live a happy life tie it to a goal not to people or things." - by Mahamta Ghandi

My life began just like most people with a childhood, dreams, goals and challenges. The goals I had in childhood helped drive me to financial success but they did not drive me to happiness. My mother made sure I knew financial success was not happiness even though most people pretend it does (to make them feel good about themselves). I was not happy working for someone else while another family raised my children. I was not happy using my talents for corporate America instead of the community that helped me "see" those same talents. I was not happy with my station in life. My family made enough money to not receive any of the benefits of low-income citizens and yet we did not have enough money to pay for all our responsibilities. We were considered middle class or what I like to say working poor, living paycheck to paycheck and going nowhere fast.

The birth of my third child was the breaking point for me. It actually was more affordable to hire a nanny than to pay for childcare for a three year old, two year old and a newborn. I thought to myself - this is crazy! What I had failed to realize is that highly educated women were not supposed to be unwed mothers. The way I saw it, I was taking the shortcut by not getting married because even if I did, it would have ended in divorce and I would have ended up in the same situation anyway. So, why put myself through all of that? My religion correctly teaches that children are to be raised in families built on the foundation of marriage where the care of the family is more important than individualistic goals or as my BFF so eloquently put it "A Muslim woman should be married."

One of my favorite classes is statistics. When I break down what Mahatma Ghandi said in this quote, I interpret it to mean an individual has a better chance of success by working in solitude to put their efforts and talents striving for a goal. People are unpredictable and should change where as things do not change as people do.

Chad Daniels wrote[37], "I have made a lot of commitments to myself in the past in regards to the direction I want to take my life. To be honest, I have failed many more times than I have succeeded. In all of these experiments to see how far I can push my growth, I have found one constant: when you have a person that you need to be accountable to, you are much more likely to stay on course and work harder on your goals. An accountability partner is someone who you trust to hold you to the standards that you set for yourself.

This is a key point. An accountability partner does not set goals for you. However, they should be the same type of person you discuss your goals with. They help keep you responsible for the goals you set, and help differentiate between legitimate shortcomings, and the lies we tell ourselves to accept straying off the path of our goals."

Muslims are striving for paradise by performing the obligations and avoiding the sins which is the ultimate goal. I am searching for people who make each other better by holding each other accountable to getting there. That is the happy life that is tied to a goal using people who hold me accountable like my future husband to get there In sha Allah.

Quote #52 "Opportunity is missed by most people because it is dressed in overalls and looks like work." by Thomas Edison

Growing up, my family watched PBS with Dr. Who and all the science fiction we could find. Of course, Star Trek, Star Wars and back to the future were classics and our favorites. Although most people become accustomed to what they have, I marvel with the next generation. They can't understand that my generation did not grow up with cell phones. We grew up with pay phones and "house" numbers. My very first computer was a keyboard that I hooked up to a TV. The world is constantly changing and this means the doors of opportunity are WIDE open! Thomas Edison said "Opportunity is missed by most people because it is dressed in overalls and looks like work."

I love working with children because in their eyes they still see opportunity in the world. My job as a parent is to empower them with tools to take advantage of this opportunity. It was my father who bought my first computer for me when I was 11 years old and my son and I have been in love with the computer ever since. Pearl S. Buck said "The young do not know enough to be prudent, and therefore they attempt the impossible -- and achieve it, generation after generation." They don't get caught up in the rat race of going nowhere fast or how some of them wear their money on the outside trying to keep up with "the joneses."

Life of 2013 looks dramatically different than life of 1983. Science Tech wrote[38], "In the past half-century, scientific and technological advances have transformed our world." In 2007 USA Today[39], listed there top 25 inventions including "Cell phones and Car phones - Were around in the 1970s, but it wasn't until 1983 that Motorola introduced the first widely available handheld cell phone. The DynaTAC 8000x weighed almost 2 pounds, but it still cost $3,995.

Laptop computers - It was about as portable as a sewing machine. But the 28-pound Compaq Portable – Compaq Computer's very first product – was the first portable IBM-compatible PC on the market. More than 53,000 sold in the year after its 1983 launch, despite a price usually topping $3,000.

Black Berries aka "crack berries" - An obscure Canadian pager company, Research In Motion, shortened attention spans around the world with the launch of the BlackBerry mobile e-mail device in 1999.

Debit cards - Ka-ching! Who needs cash when you've got a debit card? They took off after Visa launched its check card in 1995. Before then, less than 2% of Americans used debit cards. Ten years later, debit card transactions exceeded those on credit cards.

Caller ID - Bill collectors and your annoying Uncle Ned are easy to ignore with this invention introduced by BellSouth in 1984 in Orlando. Caller ID followed voice mail, an invention built a decade before to make up for declining secretarial employment.

DVDs - Americans traded all those hours rewinding video cassettes for hours watching directors kibitz about behind-the-scenes antics with the introduction of digital video discs in 1995. Consumers spent $7.4 billion on DVD rentals in 2006 up 10%. VHS rentals plummeted 74%, to $281 million.

Lithium Rechargeable Batteries - How many AAs does it take to power a laptop? Almost no one knows, thanks to the durable rechargeable battery Sony brought to market in 1991. It made its debut in a Sony camcorder – and has provided juice for laptops, cellphones, digital cameras and other portable electronics ever since.

Lettuce In A Bag - Americans discovered there's more to salad than iceberg lettuce drowning in bottled dressing after the rollout of mixed lettuce greens in a bag. Fresh Express in Salinas, Calif., made that possible by inventing a high-tech plastic bag introduced nationwide in 1989. That helped ignite a whole consumer category of portion-controlled foods, such as bagged baby carrots.

Digital Cameras - Kodak unveiled a digital camera for professionals in 1986, when consumers were still getting millions of rolls of film processed in labs. Apple followed with the first consumer version eight years later. But it wasn't until this century that cameras got affordable, driving consumers to buy a forecast 30 million this year.

iPods - Walking down the sidewalk hasn't been the same since November 2001, when Apple introduced its iconic portable digital music player. It wasn't the first player, but fans declared it the coolest and easiest to use by snapping up more than 100 million of them.

Pay At The Pump - Filling up the tank became even more self-serve when a gas station chain in Abilene, Texas, invented technology that turned the pump into a quasi-ATM."

Then Switched.com[40] added these to the list
"The Game Boy: The original Game Boy sold over 70 million units and brought us solid portable gaming.

Voice Mail: Remember tape-based answering machines?

Yeah, we're trying to forget as well.

MP3s: Say what you want about the iPod, but if it wasn't for the tiny MP3 file, we'd never be able to carry 5,000 songs in our pocket.

GPS for the masses: Sure, GPS has been around for a long time, but the death of the map on the back seat is upon us, and our safety/sanity/trees thank us.

eBay & PayPal: That junk in your garage? Someone's willing to pay for it on eBay. Trust us.
Wi-Fi: Wireless Internet was the final step toward making laptops truly portable."

Complex.com[41], pointed out some big ones like

"Hybrid Cars Made Popular By: Toyota Prius Year: 1996
The history of hybrid cars goes back to the year 1900, when legendary engineer Ferdinand Porsche (yes, the guy that started Porsche) built the Mixte which used individual wheel motors. But it wasn't until 1997 that improved lithium-ion and nickel-metal hydride battery tech allowed the first mass-produced hybrid—the Toyota Prius—to hit the streets. Though plagued with problems at first, the Prius got better and an

entire market was born. Every automaker either builds one, or plans to bring one to market. And it is easy to see why: In 2009, hybrids accounted for 2.5% of all American car sales. It is big business, kid.

Color Plasma Display Made Popular By: Fujitsu Year: 1992
It used to be that if you wanted the best possible picture from a flat screen television, you would cop a plasma. The blacks were richer, the action was faster, and the colors were brighter. We can all thank the University of Illinois for that. It developed the technology Fujitsu used to build the first color plasma display. See, Lincoln's home produced more Remember when you had to buy a special cleaner to wipe your (mouse) ball down every time it got a little grimy? If you don't, thank you for making us feel super-old. If you do, then you also remember how crazy an optical mouse was. Optical mice work using either an LED or laser diode along with a image processor to track the surface it is sliding across. Developed in the '80s by two teams—one at MIT and one at Xerox—it wasn't until 1998 when Travis N. Blalock, Richard A. Baumgartner, Thomas Hornak, and Mark T. Smith at HP Labs patented the technology that it became a hit with the masses.

LED Headlights Made Popular By: Audi Year: 2009
Light-emitting diodes (LED) have been used for taillights, turn signals, and cabin lights for some time now. With the

technology advancing to the point where an LED setup can produce more light than a traditional incandescent headlight while using less energy and producing less heat, carmakers like Audi are starting to use LED bulbs as their main source of illumination. What this means is greater, cleaner visibility, with a design way iller than anything we've seen so far."

Thomas Edison was right. This is work but it is one of the best types of work out there. It is work to make an impact on helping the human condition. They made updates with new water tanks and solar panels to "this old house" in my hometown of Philadelphia. This is meant to inspire my children to see what I see and thats a world of opportunity. Now let's see how I can use this brain to remove the outdated and shady politicians.

Quote #53 "Many hands make light work." - by John Heywood

Every other day, when my daughter and I have a difference of opinion, I say "You only have one mother" and she responds "No, I don't." Some days, she has 5 mothers - each of my Best Friends Forever (BFF) and some days she has 6 mothers - my 5 BFF's and the mother of her BFF. When I say, she is my only daughter, she says "No, I am not." Then she runs down a very familiar list of children. The village of BFF's, as I call it, is very proud of the relationships we have with one another. Sometimes being the only child can seem lonely but I learned during my youth to be a BFF to myself. Now I have a whole slew of hand picked sister girlfriends and their children.

Edmund Lee said "Surround yourself with the dreamers and the doers, the believers and the thinkers, but most of all, surround yourself with those who see the greatness within you, even when you don't see it yourself." The village includes all types of women some on the quiet side and many on the loud and crazy side. Each of us has our own path to financial wealth. We all knew that investing in the scarce resource of real estate was key and that's why the village has 2 notaries, 2 real estate agents, 1 property management company and an investor. Somehow in our "truth tables" of our youth we knew instinctively that "many hands make light work." That is why we each chose a different part of the real estate investment dream. As life unfolded and some of us became wives and all of us became mothers, our dream was deferred. We all have lifted and we climbed down the path of business ownership.

Saying that we are friends is more than a just talk. It was a verbal commitment backed up by action. Muhammad Ali is credited with saying "Friendship is the hardest thing in the world to explain. It is not something you learn in school. But if you haven't learned the meaning of friendship, you really haven't learned anything." When my house was broken into at 10pm while I was still at home, one of my friends allowed my family to stay with her until the alarm system was installed 3 days later. When my house was under construction for a month, my family including my new born son lived with another BFF. When one of the BFF's needed a new car, she knew who to turn to for the down payment. While I was working with my mentor on a Monday presentation, Tuesday training, Super Saturday and Sunday phone team, one of my BFF's was holding the fort down by taking care of the Newman children. Alexander Dumas explained correctly that "Friendship consists in forgetting what one gives and remembering what one receives." I did not know the amount of support I needed on the path to business ownership. The many hands of the village of BFF's made all the work that was required on this journey seem light. Alhamdulillah!

Quote #54 "When there is no enemy within, the enemies outside can not hurt you." - by Author Unknown

My blessing is an overflowing tank of love. When there is no more hurt, there can only be love. I have been hurt by hurt people. They say "hurt people, hurt people" but out of this pain comes compassion and that is compassion of the human, specifically African-American compassion. My experiences have made me aware of the blessings that surrounded us. Old African Proverb says "When there is no enemy within, the enemies outside can not hurt you."

People still try to hurt but I choose to look the other way and smile. Unlike the hurt people, I know I am blessed. I recognized how blessed I was in my late teens. Experiences happened that allowed me to see, later in life, that everything is made possible by the will of Allah. I was being blessed when I felt as though my behavior did not deserve the blessing. When I was 18, I was involved in a car accident that left me with a broken femur bone and sublegal hematoma. I was blessed to be alive. Four years after the accident, the resulting lawsuit netted 125,000 dollar settlement and 1,000 per month for 3 years. I was being blessed when I felt as though my behavior did not deserve the blessing. I felt like I was an F student in college that was rewarded with a new car. I was 22 at the time and was witness to the most money ever seen in my immediate family. It changed my life. I did not make good decisions with the money because I was so financially inexperienced. But the lesson I learned is that blessings come from God and not people.

If I wanted to continue being able to receive the blessings being given, I needed to change my behavior. I desired to be worthy of the blessings that were being provided by the will of Allah. Instead of being an F student, I desired to be an A student that was rewarded with a new car. Abraham Lincoln said "We can complain because rose bushes have thorns, rejoice because rose bushes have thorns." In life, we are given a choice of how to look at hardships, tests and trials. They say "Attitude determines altitude."

Every hardship, trial and test has been a blessing in disguise but during the time I was unable to "see" it. Now I choose to look for the silver linings in the rain cloud. A lot of people walk around thinking everyone else is trying to "get" them. Who cares? Our job is to strive toward being just plain "good" people who perform the obligations and avoid the sins. Bringing dislike or hate of fellow man unto our hearts brings an enemy within ourselves. That is why they say, "When there is no enemy within, the enemies outside can not hurt you." So, I choose not to retaliate or hate my fellow man. A fellow man or woman can not hurt me and choosing to hurt another brings the enemy within.

Quote #55 "It's a lot about raising the bar, increasing your expectations of yourself, to see yourself as a winner. And part of that comes from earning the respect of others through hard work." by Kris Thorson

Bruce Lee said "Knowledge will give you power, but character gives you respect." Discipline builds character. Having the discipline to use a person's blessings for self indulgent pleasure does not build character. Instead, using a person's blessings for the benefit of others with the correct intention builds character. Abraham Joshua Heschel says "Self-respect is the root of discipline: The sense of dignity grows with the ability to say no to oneself."

Merriam Webster dictionary defines respect as a feeling of admiring someone or something that is good, valuable, important, etc. It's funny because most people including the merriam webster dictionary think of respect as how other people view someone or something. In actuality, respect is what a person projects through their behavior ON TO other people. The one who disrespects another is, in actuality, disrespecting their self. Likewise, the person who respects another person respects the self. That's how one can tell what people think of their self by how they treat other people.

So what Bruce Lee's quote can be interpreted as saying is that discipline of character build self-respect. The self-respect of a persons' discipline is projected onto other people. No one has to earn respect from anyone else. The discipline of a person is how self-respect is acquired and obtained. That is also projected to other people.

Lao Tzu said "When you are content to be simply yourself and don't compare or compete, everyone will respect you." In other words, trying to compete with others shows weakness of character in the self. Other people will notice that you have elevated to a higher ground. You are no longer participating in the crabs in a barrel mentality. That is what Kris Thorson also said in "It's a lot about raising the bar, increasing your expectations of yourself, to see yourself as a winner. And part of that comes from earning the respect of others through hard work." Discipline allows a person to raise the expectations of self so they can start to believe that they are a winner. When a person can believe that they deserve to be victorious, their efforts will begin to match their belief.

I will end this book of wisdom about the lessons I learned from Moms, Mentors and Mistakes on a quote that sums up the journey that brought me here. Mary Rubin said "Happiness is the highest form of self-respect. A person who allows himself to be happy shows his self-respect." Please make the choice to be disciplined and focused in your personal search for happiness In sha Allah.

Index

1. http://www.irs.gov/uac/Is-Your-Hobby-a-For-Profit-Endeavor%3F
2. http://www.thefreedictionary.com/hustle
3. http://www.forbes.com/sites/sap/2012/08/09/what-is-marketing
4. http://www.financialsocialwork.com/delving-more-deeply-into-the-poverty-mindset
5. http://www.danijohnson.com/2010/6-keys-to-break-off-a-poverty-mindset
6. http://www.psychologytoday.com/blog/adventures-in-dating/201306/workplace-romance-motives, (Horan & Chory, 2011, p. 565)
7. newmannetworks.freshbooks.com/refer/www
8. http://smallbusiness.foxbusiness.com/starting-a-business/2012/05/18/tory-johnson-spark-hustle/
9. https://www.openforum.com/articles/plans-are-nothing-but-planning-is-everything
10. http://www.elephantjournal.com/2012/12/wealth-is-a-state-of-mind-claire-amber
11. http://positivepsychologynews.com/search-by/image-maps/positive-emotions/gratitude-and-forgiveness
12. http://www.salrachele.com/webarticles/forgivenessandgratitude.htm
13. http://www.livescience.com/14152-destructive-human-behaviors-bad-habits.html
14. http://www.ritholtz.com/blog/2012/01/small-business-successfailure-rates
15. http://hiroboga.com/blog/soul-of-business/grow-your-business-grow-yourself-risk-complexity-and-creative-capacity
16. http://lifehacker.com/5898661/the-ultimate-inspiration-is-the-deadline
17. http://thekidcounselor.com/articles/the-problem-with-labeling-children
18. http://www.johnmaxwell.com/blog/the-law-of-the-lid
19. http://newamericamedia.org/2010/09/educators-system-sets-up-black-boys-to-fail.php
20. http://smallbusiness.foxbusiness.com/starting-a-business/2012/05/18/tory-johnson-spark-hustle
21. http://www.stle.org/resources/articledetails.aspx?did=1070
22. http://www.forbes.com/sites/kevinkruse/2013/04/09/what-is-leadership
23. http://bridgecolumn.proboards.com/index.cgi?board=read&action=d

isplay&thread=134

24. http://danwaldschmidt.com/2012/06/business/why-doing-the-right-thing-is-always-the-right-thing

25. http://www.positivityblog.com/index.php/2008/12/03/why-you-should-do-the-right-thing-and-how-to-do-it

26. http://www.psychologytoday.com/blog/emotional-fitness/201103/10-ways-feel-better-about-yourself

27. http://www.ted.com/talks/richard_st_john_s_8_secrets_of_success.html

28. http://www.asmp.org/strictlybusiness/2011/05/all-business-is-personal/#.Un77qvlJNsE

29. http://highered.mcgraw-hill.com/sites/dl/free/0072400722/31216/Ch01Adler.pdf

30. http://www.inc.com/geoffrey-james/what-is-success-better-definition.html

31. http://www.forbes.com/sites/kevinkruse/2013/04/09/what-is-leadership

32. http://www.amazon.com/The-Power-Focus-Jack-Canfield/dp/0091876508

33. http://www.reliableplant.com/Read/12675/communication-most-important-key-to-leadership-success

34. http://businesspaths.net/Articles/12/people-quit-their-boss-not-their-job

35. http://www.psychologytoday.com/blog/the-good-life/201109/goal-setting-dont-pick-the-low-hanging-fruit

36. http://www.wikihow.com/Build-Trust

37. http://buildthefire.com/the-power-of-an-accountability-partner/

38. http://www.dailymail.co.uk/sciencetech/article-2449468/Sony-Walkman-zip-Past-centurys-100-inventions.html

39. http://usatoday30.usatoday.com/news/top25-inventions.htm

40. http://www.switched.com/2007/05/21/top-25-tech-inventions-of-the-last-25-years

41. http://www.complex.com/tech/2010/08/the-50-greatest-technological-inventions

www.ingramcontent.com/pod-product-compliance
Lightning Source LLC
Chambersburg PA
CBHW031932190326
41519CB00007B/498